Land and water reform: The basis for changing rural society from poverty to prosperity

Sandeep Deshmukh

&

Vilasrao Salunkhe

Original Draft: 1997

Revised: 2020

Land and water reform: The basis for changing rural society from poverty to prosperity

---

First Edition, October 2020

ISBN 978-93-5419-331-6

First published in India in 2020 by Sandeep Deshmukh

Authored by Sandeep Deshmukh and Vilasrao Salunkhe

Set by Sandeep Deshmukh

Printed in India

Land and water reform:

The basis for changing the rural society from poverty to prosperity

In the service of citizens of India

Contents

Preface

'Land and water reform: The basis for changing rural society from poverty to prosperity'. This is a book that took birth in the summer of 1997. It is a product of intellectual labor of two persons with divergent social, professional and academic background. Late Vilasrao Salunkhe, son of a soldier from the hardy farming communities of western Maharashtra was an engineer who had set up a successful instrumentation industry in Pune. I was a city lad who had first seen villages from a distance during brief, magic filled vacations to a maternal uncle who had a government job in rural area. My true engagement with villages began during my first stint with the science education program of the Tata Institute of Fundamental Research. Then it went on with an increasing crescendo. In the brief but intense collaboration with Late Vilasarao, he came across a gentleman, soft spoken person with excellent skills in Marathi, an intense gaze and convictions which were not easily shakable. We did not bring out this book while Vilasrao was alive, and I have no guilt about it. This is an unfinished book because it is quite likely that my late comrade would have wanted to further work on this book, in today's changed circumstances. I did not want to work further on the book because of my liberal view that development is not only about economics but also about culture and social structures. I stopped the project and unfortunately my comrade died in 2003. I had decided not to publish this manuscript after his death. What changed my mind? My experience of last twenty three years since the birth of this book has shown the persistence of physical poverty in deep and large pockets of India in spite of the political claims of splendid economic growth. My present perception is part subjective and part based on data. So I wonder if that alternative perspective on development jointly authored by Vilasrao and me could be brought back to the now weak but essential discussion on nature and objectives of development. This is undoubtedly justice to my dead friend too. I hope this book will rekindle interest of academia, development practitioners and policy makers in the approach developed by Vilasrao on equity in distribution of natural resources. I have also added excerpts from the original draft in appendix 4, which Vilasrao did not agree with and I had exclusively written without his inputs. The book is going to be palatable to the reader in the context of 1990s, and attempt to blindly tailor analysis and measures to present scenario may misfire.

Sandeep Deshmukh
Mumbai, 19th December 2020

Introduction

The present book came into existence against the background of a transforming India almost at the far end of the last century. Since early 1980s Indian elite had started admitting the failures of the socialistic model of development. They were gradually capitulating to the market driven economic model. When viewed superficially, the book presented a contrast to the increasingly popular noise of market driven economics. The theme of equitable distribution of land and water reads like an orthodox Marxist proposal, but it is not. The book simply speaks about the right of multitudes of hardworking agriculture dependent masses to dignified livelihood. It does not advocate doles and politics of poverty. On the contrary, the book seeks creation of self-organized, professional communities of farmers. It looks at the effective management of distribution of water as a precondition for larger social development of India. The book points out that access of majority people to land will not suffice to achieve the goal of stable development. While I am introducing the reader to the innards of this small book, farmers from northwest corners of India are knocking on the doors of her capital. Perhaps concealed behind the war slogans of these farmers are the massive contradictions and deep fault lines in our contemporary social-economic fabric. Our book attempted to point out some of those critical fault lines twenty three years ago, and I personally feel that they are still there; though, in the interim we have at least tried to learn better methods of managing our resources.

The book is organized in four chapters, three supplementary notes and four appendices. The first chapter 'the contemporary social scenario' exposes the demographic, economic and social forces that characterized the agrarian crisis of India when it was a five decades old political entity limited by the principles of universal suffrage. It tries to define India's agrarian problem in a globally hierarchized economic network as it was in the last decade of last century. The chapter traces the organic link between the urban and rural poverty. The chapter questions the functionality of the established policy perspective on agriculture and rural poverty as the decision makers continued to take measures that reinforced the fault lines instead of mitigating those. The authors asserted that the problems of environmental degradation, urban migration, rural deprivation and escalating costs of farm operations are intertwined and cannot be understood in isolation.

The second chapter 'deconstructing the contemporary history' focuses on the function of policy as a tool of translating a perspective into a plan. It traces the historical roots of the 'India as a young, marginalized and competing state' narrative of the Indian political elite which intensely dominated all efforts of development till seventies. The chapter discusses the ideological pitfalls of the practice of fragmented development thinking of Indian state. The fragmented perspective led to fragmented plans. One of the effects of this practice is low agricultural growth and unequal distribution of resources. The chapter discusses the disparities between regions in terms of potential and actual land under cultivation and access to water. The discussion proceeds with the help of two cases – Maharashtra and China.

The third chapter 'salient features of the new social policy of equitable distribution of land and water' looks at the possibility of new organizational forms for rural development. There is a revisit to the philosophy of Gram Swaraj of Mohandas Gandhi and we extend the approach of 'self-reliant community' to the idea of sustainable management of natural resources.

The fourth chapter 'the alternative development policy (directions)' deals with the specific operational constraints faced by the official development perspective in India till then. Each of the main constraints, namely, problems of growth driven economy, macro perspective of development, centralized governance and sector based approach are spelt out. Then the chapter presents the ideological and operational outline of the alternative development policy of equitable distribution of land and water.

The three notes briefly deal with the issues of dilemma of Green Revolution; the social science construct of community as a basis of development management; and the paradox of State Power versus People's Power.

There are four appendices in the book. The first appendix gives elaborate treatment to the theoretical issues of economic and social paradigms of development. First it looks at the feasibility of the traditional village serving as a unit of a modern system of equity based distribution of land and water. Then the problem of emergence of a capitalist class of farmers out of the remnants of the feudal system has been discussed. The emergence of an assertive capitalist class in rural area is accompanied by marginalization of small landholders. Still India did not present a uniform landholding pattern in the 1990s. The pockets of feudal landholding, quite sizable in northern states, remained. This collage of regional landholding patterns posed a major challenge to solve the problem of equitable distribution of economic resources, and I think it continues to do so even now. Third, the scope for salvaging water shortages has been discussed briefly with respect to the precipitation patterns of Maharashtra. The fourth and fifth points together discuss the gross failures of the economic paradigm of development and the possibility of equity in land and water overcoming the impact of these failures.

The second appendix presents statistical data related to landholdings, land use and irrigation for the state of Maharashtra. The data is arranged in twenty three tables.

The third appendix briefly discusses the Pani Panchayat Model of equitable distribution.

The fourth appendix includes notes that the main author had prepared for the main body of the book. However, due to difference of opinion about the purpose of the book, he kept these points as supplementary notes. Vilasrao Salunkhe had no contribution to these notes and perhaps did not agree with these arguments. Some of the important points deserve mention – maximization of irrigation potential in India; transition of the pre-colonial revenue system into the colonial one and rubble left in the wake of it, etc.

There is an appropriate bibliography. These documents were extensively studied, jointly and individually, by both the authors to arrive at our convergent insights.

In the end, the surviving author who happens to be the main author may like to remind the reader to interpret the book in its historical context that existed nearly a quarter century ago. The authors were interested in an objective introduction to the structures underlying the façade of poverty, low employment and under productivity in India and in no way aspired to favor any ideology or political system. Same policies and institutional structures can exist under different political systems, as it was rightly observed by a soviet era scholar L. Blyakhman (1977) with respect to technology.

Chapter I: The contemporary social scenario

This is the 50th year of India's independence and the occasion is being celebrated with lots of ardor in the country. It is to be noted against this mood of celebration that the country's population which is already touching the grand figure of 1,000 million is going to reach the limit of 1,700 million in the year 2050; and then we will be topping the list of nations as the most populous country. Indeed, we will leave China way behind in this respect around this time as our population is increasing at a rate of 18 million per year at present.

1. Being part of the global hierarchy

The rapidity in scientific development, technological advancement, and building of massive infrastructure of production deeply affects the social fabric of a society. The countries of the world are divided into three categories, namely, the developed, the newly developed and the developing ones. A rapid industrialization changes the distribution of population in the urban and rural areas. It has been almost a rule in all countries that the higher the level of industrialization the more the population in the urban areas. Thus, one finds that the countries falling in the category of the developed nations have very little population living in the rural areas (In most of the developed countries the rural population has decreased to 3 - 15 % of the total population).

India belongs to the category of developing countries. In the beginning of her independence, the population living in rural parts was 90 % of the total population which has been reduced to 63 % at present. The change was effected due to rapid industrial growth and concomitant rise in the urban population. According to one estimate, it will be reduced to 60% in future. Though this presents a picture of consistent increase in the urban population, yet it must be noted that due to the effect of the population increasing in multiples, the total population living in rural areas at present is more than double the total population of the country at the time of independence. Therefore, in spite of some part of the rural population migrating towards the urban areas in the coming future; still the pressure of population in the rural areas will be great.

India was known as an agricultural country at the time of independence; however, with increasing proportion of industrial sector and with increase in trade with the globally located centers we have already stepped into the process of global economic liberalization. As a consequence, the share of the population depending on agriculture for livelihood in the total population of the country has started dwindling. For example, the annual per capita income of the population relying on agriculture for livelihood was Rs.926 in Maharashtra in the year 1994-95, while it was Rs.13,887 per capita per annum from non-agricultural sources for population not depending on agriculture (with reference to the price index of 1980-81)[i].

Thus, the economic development of India in the last fifty years had different consequences for two distinct parts of our society. There is a widening gap in the economic status of the urban and rural population in spite of the impressive trend of economic development at the national and state level. The national planning is projecting a growth rate of 6-8 % for the near future; however, past experience does not assure that there will be an equitable distribution of benefits from this economic growth. The process of weakening of the economic strength of the rural masses is indeed being ensured through adopting the modern technology that is reducing a mass of employable population to state of absence of gainful employment. The problem of unemployment due to inequitable distribution of economic growth is getting compounded by a degradation of environment because of soil erosion.

2. Social stratification in contemporary Indian society

The inequality in Indian polity is further complicated due to further stratification within the urban and rural divisions. Today each of the two divisions is again divided into sharply demarcated economic and social strata. The urban population, for example, is sharply cut into the upper class of senior bureaucrats, political satraps, businessmen, industrialists and those employed in the top rung of the industrial corporate sector, the middle class, and the poor comprising working class and the unemployed or marginally employed ones. Similarly the rural population is divided into those with sizable landholding and having a hold over irrigation facilities and other agriculture inputs; the small and the marginal farmers and the landless. The small and marginal farmers as well as the landless laborers form a major part of the Indian rural population.

The poor of the urban and rural areas exist as if they are bound to the same historical fate. They are continuously subjected to the crisis of economic and cultural survival. There is an organic relationship between the poor of urban and rural areas. Indeed the displaced poor coming from the vast mass of small and marginal farmers and the landless laborers form the major bulk of the lower rungs of the social hierarchy in the urban areas. Furthermore, these economic divisions are vertically cut into a social stratification based on caste and ethnic identities. The economic and social identities crosscutting each other at different levels produce a very intricate pattern of stratification.

The phenomenon of social stratification in the contemporary Indian society could be summarized as follows.

- A steady growth in the urban population which has a close relation with the process of displacement of members of the lower rungs of the rural population, leading towards the widening urban and rural divide

- Urbanization has resulted in concentration of certain classes in the urban areas, that is, the upper class, the middle class of the salaried; and the working class.

- The caste and religious groups in the traditional social order have been transformed into competing ethnic groups due to spread of the democratic process.

- There is a steady increase in the number and proportion of small farmers, marginal farmers, and the landless laborers in the country. This talks about the growing polarization in the rural society. The rift between the large and small farmers is growing steadily. Here the category of large farmers includes those who are relatively a minority in the total population of the farmers yet control largest or major portions of the land in the country. This rift is with relation to control over the means of irrigation; access to other farm inputs; and the viability of the agricultural produces in the market.

- The economic inequalities in the rural areas again get accentuated by the processes of political patronage and caste based exploitation.

- The tribal groups are driven to join the lower ranks of the urban and rural social order, a process which has triggered off a series of violent conflicts between the tribal and non-tribal groups. The struggle of tribal population in most cases does not find a slot in the economic hierarchy; but on the contrary it gets transformed in a struggle to keep independent cultural identity.

3. <u>The farmer hangs onto the tail</u>

Therefore, the contemporary Indian society is characterized by inequitable distribution of the fruits of development; and social stratification that reinforces inequitable distribution of fruits of development. These problems are rooted as much as in our post – independence policy of development as much as they are steeped in our 'history' spread over the ages.

The conventional policy of development emphasized the primacy of the economic growth over any other form of social development. Therefore, there was an obvious insistence on industrialization and commercialization including that of agriculture. Industrialization brought with it urbanization. The urban society has three types of needs, namely (1) essential needs; (2) needs for making life more comfortable above subsistence; and (3) needs adding to the indulgence and opulence of a few.

In order to meet the first category of needs, the farmer is required to input costly resources in agriculture; for which again he has to depend on the urban based industrial production systems. Again the produce obtained from such a cost-intensive agriculture has to be transported to the urban markets which itself is a costly affair. Therefore, the strategy is to drive the farmer to use less land and maximum water and costly inputs for production. Obviously, very few farmers can manage to organize the resources efficiently in order to meet this requirement. Consequently, the mass of farmers are alienated from the industrial system and increasingly dependent on rainfall for production. This leads to degradation of environment. The phenomenon is a manifestation of the deeply entrenched attitude of indifference in our society at large and particularly, the policy makers towards need to plan development and use of land and water resources in an integrated manner.

Therefore, a rational approach to defining the form and content of development would be to scrutinize the premises of the established development policy in a historical perspective. Indeed, it is an essential task in the process of creating an egalitarian social order. We will look into this aspect of the problem later.

4. Political populism drowns the need for introspection

Therefore, those concerned about the need for a sustainable scheme of development in this country know that the problem of social reconstruction towards an egalitarian order is a complex one with social, economic and political dimensions. The complexity of the problem itself calls for a 'political will' to evolve an agenda of social change. History tells us that major social changes with major political implications have been effected by political organizations. However, the performance of political organizations in our country appears dismal on this front. The democratic multiparty system is in operation in the states and at the center in the country. If equal opportunity is offered to everybody in society, then with the help of economic development, employment and enrichment of environment, we could overcome the problem of poverty; yet all political parties are busy competing with each other announcing populist programs that require increasing expenditure. Thus, irrespective of the increasing expenditure on the innumerable government programs, we are not able to overcome the problem of poverty, unemployment and degradation of environment.

Chapter II: Deconstructing the contemporary history

The emergence of a new perspective of development is a synthetic process which is characterized by a criticism of the existing systems of thought. The criticism focuses on the internal contradictions in the competing systems and in turn proposes to resolve those contradictions. We propose to do it partially here as well, with the modest aspiration of scrutinizing the aspects of established view of development in India as far as it has a direct bearing upon the formal policy of development. The focus on 'policy' is decided on basis of the very fundamental function of policy as an instrument of transforming a perspective into a plan. Therefore, we emphasize this outlook with the understanding that there is a dialectical relationship between the policy perspectives of the State and the existing social and economic conditions in society. With respect to this outlook, we would focus on three dimensions of development planning and implementation, viz.

1. Ideological premises of the conventional policy of development

2. Policy implementation process

3. Social and economic implications of the policy implementation process

Each dimension is discussed in details here.

4. <u>Ideological premises of the conventional policy of development</u>

The leadership of newly independent India spoke about the need to establish a Welfare State that would be committed to providing services satisfying the basic needs of its citizens such as food, clothing and shelter. On the other hand, they understood the political importance of having a high economic growth rate, and they looked upon the State as the only force that could mobilize the resources necessary to achieve this stage. This model of the State was equally rooted in the apparently antagonistic 'socialist state' and 'welfare state' perspectives. The political ideology emerging from this synthesis strongly emphasized the control of production and market systems with the belief that this is necessary in order to achieve an egalitarian social order. This was thought to be an essential measure to ensure equitable distribution of economic benefits among different sections of society.

On the other hand, the interest of political leadership in India in economic growth was rooted in the political circumstances of the decades of 50s and 60s. Our policy – makers strongly felt that if we had to survive in the international political arena dominated by the 'northern block' of countries, we must become economically strong (which implied economic independence). Thus, they emphasized the need (i) to strengthen our industrial base; and (ii) to augment agricultural production. Both these thrusts were supposed to ensure high economic growth. Another significant aspect of this thinking was that high economic growth would percolate down to all strata of society and this would lead to elevation of material conditions of living of the population in general. The improvement in material living conditions, in turn, was supposed to enhance social and cultural development of the population.

5. Policy implementation

a. Fragmented planning and alienation of masses

These premises have shaped the planning practice in India. The planning perspective in our country looks upon the life of the people as a fragmented entity. In the planning rooted in such a perspective, links mostly exist vertically between specialized programs at the bottom and the decision makers at the top. No horizontal links are conceived between different dimensions of the life conditions of the population. Therefore, as far as people in the development process are concerned, they are not supposed to figure out the relationship between the significance of change in one sphere of life with another. This setup even blocks the direct communication among the participants of the development programs. These factors cumulatively lead to alienation of masses from the mainstream of development processes. This situation has led to a dependence of large sections of population on the government and other centrally operating agencies to satisfy even their basic needs. This has resulted in lack of compatibility between resource inputs and outputs.

b. Relegating agriculture to the background

The patterns of development in general indicate that agriculture is fast losing its share in the economic growth; as well as the access to the fiscal and physical resources required for expected performance in the country. This is a complex phenomenon which is determined by our very perception of development. We are yet to come out of the spell of the *mantra* 'rate of economic growth determines the pace of development'. Therefore, we see the inability of agriculture to stand on firm ground in face of the competition from the urban oriented sectors of development.

Firstly, agriculture has lost position to industry and commerce with respect to the share in the economic growth. Ironically this has happened in spite of engagement of an overwhelming majority of our productive population in agriculture. Secondly, the very structure of rural production systems has resulted in the assets being siphoned off and diversion of the resources meant for the rural poor. This has especially taken place through the urban oriented market systems. Thirdly, the irrigation sector of the country has already started feeling the pinch of the circumstances arising out of the demands and expectations imposed by the new economic order as well as out of its own performance. Experts have observed that the end of the potential for physical expansion of irrigation is the bottom line of the impending irrigation crisis in the country. The problem is further compounded by the growing competition for water resources from the non-irrigation sector. One needs to imagine the consequences of this phenomenon for the health of agriculture sector of the country. The social disaster that this pattern would bring to the rural poor if it continues unabated might blow off the bottom of civic order of our society.

6. Social and economic implications of the policy implementation

The fragmented perspective of development culminating into isolated treatment to agriculture has already induced disparities in that sector which has in turn created fissures in the social fabric of our country. It may be reiterated here that the major reason for social and economic inequality in the country is the unequal distribution of land. However, nowhere the policy makers took into account the fact that mere distribution of non-irrigated land is not a sufficient condition for economic growth. It is amply clear now that availability of irrigation can make even a small piece of land highly productive. Therefore, the need for now is to approach the problem of development on the basis of integration of the policies of distribution and use of land and water resources and development of the irrigated area. Where do we stand today with regard to the last point.

a. The disparities in agriculture at the national level

The net sown area (hectare) per farmer is different for different states. The average N.S.A. for the country is 1.30 hectares. It is 2.2, 2.2, 2, 1.9.1.8, 0.9, 0.8 and 0.7 hectares for Punjab, Kerala, Gujarat, Rajasthan, Maharashtra, West Bengal, Uttar Pradesh and Bihar respectively.

The Net Sown Area of the country is 141 million hectares, and the gross area under cropping is 183 million hectares. The net irrigated area in the net area under cropping is 64 million hectares. Thus, the percentage of Net Area under Irrigation in the Net Area under cropping is 35 % at the national level. The difference in the proportion of area under irrigation is conspicuous for different states of the country. The percentage of the area under irrigation is 95 % in Punjab, 78 % in Haryana, 57% in Uttar Pradesh, 47 % in Tamil Nadu, 27 % in Gujrat, 22 % in West Bengal, and 16 % in Maharashtra.

Even the yield of food grains and other crops differs according to availability of irrigation between the states in the country. The net yield of food grains per hectare is 1,442 kilograms at the national level. The amount for the same variable is 1,267 kilograms in Maharashtra. The average yield of cotton per hectare is 240 kilograms for India while it is 545 kilograms in Punjab and 123 kilograms in Maharashtra. The per capita yield of food grains at the national level is 202 kilograms while it is 918 kilograms in Punjab and 147 kilograms in Maharashtra.

The statistics offered above proves that mere expansion of area under cultivation is not sufficient to raise levels of production; on the contrary availability of irrigation is a precondition for that. The production of food grains has reached from 50 million at the time of independence to 196 million tons at present in India. In spite of a two and half time increase in the population during this period we have not only been able to become self-sufficient but even export some of the food grains and other agricultural produces. We are able to achieve this spectacular task because of the combining of agriculture development with development of irrigation.

One is confronted with the paradox that on the one hand the agricultural production and area under irrigation have increased; yet on the other hand, one finds that an increasing proportion of rural population is living below the poverty line. A proper framework for discussing the manifestation of this paradox is provided by the phenomenon of commercialization of agriculture which is called as Green Revolution in the popular parlance. Some major dimensions of it have been summarized in the Note 1. This condition may be alleviated only through redistribution of land and water resources on the principle of equity, proper planning and utilization of the two resources combined with local manpower. Indeed it has been proved that in those areas where 60% of the total land under cultivation is irrigated, the proportion of population living below poverty line is negligible. The relevance of this proposition may be checked out with the example of land and water related conditions in the state of Maharashtra here.

b. Potential for equitable distribution of land and water resources: A case of Maharashtra

The state of Maharashtra is considered as one of the most progressive states in the country, and with the largest industrial base in India. The people of the state have always proved to be trendsetters with respect to a number of progressive changes. As it happened in case of western countries whose experience of development, at least partially if not entirely, helped the developing countries in defining their own course of development; perhaps the same may be said with respect to the role of the state of Maharashtra for India. The problems faced by the people of the state while bringing about certain social and economic changes may sound a note of caution for other states as they might try to avoid the same mistakes in the same situations in near future. With the vast base of land, water and other natural resources at disposal, the state could have provided better living conditions to the various sections of the population if suitably calibrated policy was followed with a mission to attain social development. The case of that state is discussed here to illustrate the need for equitable distribution of land and water resources and integrated planning of land, water and manpower.

(i) The inequitable distribution of land and water resources between the areas of the state

The total geographical area of the state of Maharashtra is 30.70 million hectares. The area is spread between the coastal belt of Konkan on the west to the plains of Vidarbha in the east. This area has been divided into thirty districts. The geographical area of the state is divided into three categories, namely, (a) forest, (b) waste land not under cultivation, and (c) agricultural land under cultivation. The total area of 30.70 million hectares is divided into these three categories as follows – forest approximately 20% (6 million hectares), waste land approximately 20% (6 million hectares) and agricultural land under cultivation approximately 60% (18 million hectares).

The proportion of the three types of land differs drastically in the different districts when compared to the proportion of the state. Land under forest is as little as 1-3 % in the districts of Ratnagiri, Solapur, Jalna, Parbhani, Beed, Osmanabad and Latur. It is in the range of 3-8%in the districts of Sindhudurg, Sangli, Aurangabad, and Buldhana. There are some districts with 10 to 20% land under forest. The land under forest is 28 to 75% in the total area of the districts of Nagpur, Bhandara, Chandrapur and Gadchiroli[ii]. Very little of the land under forest is properly maintained in the state and very little portion of this land is productive. The wasteland other than the land under forest is divided into three types, namely, land not available for cultivation, land not meant for cultivation and waste land.

Land under forest, the net sown area except the waste land make up for 60 % of the total geographical area of the state (i.e. 18 million hectares). In some parts of the state, this area is used for biennial cropping. The area under biennial cropping was 3.3 million hectares in 1994-95, while the net sown area was 21.40 million hectares.

There is a wide range of the ratio of net sown area to the total geographical area in different districts of the state. It is less than 30 % in the districts of Thane, Raigad, Ratnagiri, Sindhudurg, and Gadchiroli. In some other districts, it is 40-50% while in some it is 50-70%.

The per capita agricultural land available is 0.40 hectares if one matches the total rural population of the state with the total agricultural area of the state; however, it differs in different districts. It is 0.20 hectares in five districts, between 0.40 hectares to 0.60 hectares in 13 districts, and 0.20 to 0.40 hectares in the remaining twelve districts.

The total rural population of the state is 62% (48.40 million) and the population of farmers and agricultural laborers is 46% (18.40 million) of the total rural population.

Irrigation is available on a very small portion of the total net sown area of 18 million hectares. Irrigation was available only on 14% (2.5 million hectares) of the total net sown area in 1994-95. The total irrigated area under biennial cropping was 3.3 million hectares in the same year. The sources for irrigation consisted of water from underground sources, canal irrigation of major, medium and small irrigation projects, and lift irrigation schemes along the rivers and tanks.

The proportion of irrigated area is between 1% and 5% in 11 districts. It is between 5% and 10% in 5 districts, while it is 20% in some of the remaining districts and between 20% and 30% in others.

The difference in the availability of irrigation facilities between districts is also visible between tehsils in the highly irrigated districts. For example, the total irrigated area in the total agricultural area of Pune district is 22%, yet it is only 1% to 4% in four tehsils; 12% in three tehsils; while it is 20% to 38% in the remaining six tehsils.

If the use of the irrigated area is compared for the entire state of Maharashtra, then it occurs that gross disparities exist between districts. Of the total water available, 60% is used for cultivation of sugarcane alone[iii]. Sugarcane is cultivated only on 3% of the total agricultural land. The disparities become acute when one moves down to the level of districts. There is a general trend that in those places where there is 25% irrigated area, there as well only 20% farmers take a larger share of water, while 40% receive very little and another 40% receive do not receive any share at all.

(ii) Unequal distribution of land and water – the major factor of social stratification

According to the agricultural census of 1990 – 91, in Maharashtra state the total number of landholders was 9.47 million. The census also pointed out that the land under cultivation available to the different categories of landholders - on the basis of the size of landholding - was not distributed equally. The average landholding is 2.2 hectares. Against this background, the number of farmers with small and marginal landholding is 6 million in the total number of landholders (they constitute 64% of the total number of landholders). They control total land of 5.5 million hectares (27% of the total land available for cultivation). In contrast to this, the landholders in the medium and large range of farm size make up 14% of the total number of cultivators and yet they control 9.4 million hectares of land (48% of the total cultivable land).

The area under irrigation was 2.63 million hectares in 1990-91 and this is 11.52 % of the total cultivable land. 2.94 million Landholders from the total number of landholders have benefitted from this provision of irrigation and their proportion in the total number of landholders is 22%. This indicates that 88% of the net sown area in the state and 78% landholders have not benefitted from irrigation at all.

The economic survey by the rural development department of that state has shown that 7 million families are living under poverty line. This number is 72% of the total population living in rural area of Maharashtra. At the time of the survey, families with an annual income below Rs.11,000/- were considered as living below poverty line. The new survey of poverty is going to be conducted under the leadership of the district collectors. The limit of poverty line has been fixed at annual income of Rs.21,000/- per family in the new survey. As well as, a farmer with 5 hectares of non-irrigated cultivable land or 2.5 hectares of irrigated cultivable land would be treated as above the poverty line.

(iii) Can we learn a few things from the food revolution of China?

The Nehru Age was dominated by the slogan of brotherhood between India and China. It came to an end with the border conflict between the two countries in 1962 and was restored in the 1980s. The two countries together make up for 35% of the total population of mankind. The population of China was 1238 million and that of India was 931 million in 1995. The urban population is 30% and 28 % of the total population in China and India respectively. It has been projected by population experts that the population of India will overtake that of China in the year 2025. The overall picture of development is far better in China when compared to India's record. For example, both the countries have almost the same per capita national annual income. However, the difference between various sections of population with respect to distribution of income is reducing in China, while exactly the opposite is happening in India. The population living under poverty line is almost nearly 50% in India while it has been reduced to a small 7% in China. With respect to the other aspects of the quality of life as well, the Chinese have taken long strides ahead of India. For example, the percentage of literate population in China is 80% while it is only 52% in India. The production of food grains of China was 480 million tons while that of India was 190 million tons in the year 1996. This happened in spite of the fact that India holds more land under cultivation than China, i.e. 141 million hectares in India and 100 million hectares in China. This shows that India has 0.3 hectares of cultivated land per head of rural population while China has only 0.1 hectares.

It has been proved in different parts of the world that poverty and unemployment feed each other. This is particularly true about the rural population. In India, we are confronted with a strange situation made up of vast tracts of land with potential for higher productivity either being underutilized or grossly misused. Irrigation as a major factor in the proper utilization of land has been proved by many examples like that of countries like Israel and China. We will compare the Chinese situation with that of India as both the countries have a number of common geopolitical factors shaping their destiny as well as they are both faced with similar kind of problems related to their vast populations.

The Chinese have literally transformed their agriculture system from an unprofitable wreck to a profitable enterprise through the integrated land and water management program at national level. The program has been implemented at the level of each village. The Chinese irrigation policy is based on the premise that irrigation is essential for agriculture like blood to human body. The total expanse of land in China is vast and there are number of complexities involved in the situation pertaining to land under cultivation, availability of water, geographical structure and economic conditions. The Chinese have realized that perhaps one could tide over the crises unleashed by the recurrent draughts through construction of small irrigation projects, yet the permanent solution to the draught with deep impact which is always looming behind the Chinese economy could be controlled only through large irrigation projects. Therefore they have created an efficient network of large, medium and small sized irrigation projects that enabled them to increase the agriculture production manifold.

The bottom-line of this system of irrigation projects is made up of the efficient institutional setup created for the integrated use of land and water resources as well as manpower. This is illustrated with a number of efficient irrigation projects in that country. The illustrations selected here present a picture of irrigation management in both macro and micro perspective.

1. <u>Irrigation is the lifeline of the nation:</u> The Chinese government gives utmost importance to water conservation. They consider water supply to agriculture as the most vital aspect, and therefore, one finds an emphasis on the policy of expansion of irrigated area. The irrigated area of China was 48

million hectares till the end of 1990; and this constituted nearly 50% of the total area under cultivation. Hubei province has 2.61 million hectares of land under irrigation and that forms 74% of the total area under cultivation in that province. In all 27 major projects, 223 medium sized projects and 6,000 small irrigation projects have been completed in that province.

2. The village level irrigation project in the Shangdong province: The small irrigation projects are implemented by the village on a large scale in China. One estimate tells us that 55% of total cultivable land is covered under these small projects in the entire country, while in the Shangdong province the proportion of such land is 95%. There were radical changes made in the village irrigation system as a part of the agrarian reforms of 1980. The new policy dictated that the farmer should have freedom of production and the family should be considered as the unit of production, yet the facilities for water supply and execution of the irrigation project were kept under the purview of the collective management.

3. Yanging irrigation project: Another example is from Gunagdong province in south China. In this province the Yanging irrigation project was completed in 1962. The targeted area under irrigation is 2,133 hectares while the actual area under cultivation is 1,086 hectares. The total population in the area is 60,000 of which 50,000 are in the rural area. There are 30,000 farmers in the total rural population. Before the project was started, the total land under irrigation was only 20% and the yield per hectare was 10 Kilograms. There was no possibility of cultivating rice in the fields. Now, because of the irrigation facility, rice is regularly cultivated. The rice yield was at its peak in 1993 with total production of 12,500 tons of rice (i.e. 8 tons per hectare) in this irrigation district. After that a few crops have been introduced in the area adding annual income worth of Chinese Yuan 2,000 (equivalent to Indian Rupees 7,000) to the regular income per farmer. The farmers benefitting from the project only manage the later. These and many other programs have proved that management of irrigation projects is efficient whenever they are directly looked after by the farmers benefitting from these. The programs have a high degree of flexibility with respect to water distribution and total management structure.

4. The Zhugqu area in Gansu province - saving the water resources: The irrigation district along the western canal is well developed since the time of the '1949' revolution. The government invested 35 million Yuan for these developments while the farmers another 6 million Yuan. The investment by the farmers was in the form of contribution of one million labor days. This enabled enhancement of the irrigated area from 70,000 μ to 220,000 μ in 1949. A protective shield of trees has been created in this district through

planting along the farm boundaries and at other sites since the air is extremely dry here. The average rainfall in this region is only 123 millimeters and the total evaporation due to air is 2,000 millimeters which is very low compared to other parts of the country. Therefore, water is supplied from the distantly located Black River (Ruo Shui) in this area. Consequently, food grains production has increased 32 times in this region. Even one notices a broadening of the range of crops as farmers have started cultivating new items like wheat, maize, soybean, and vegetables.

Modern agricultural technology has been used in the region to make economic use of each cubic meter. 3,000 to 10,000 kilograms of organic manure is used along with 30 to 150 kilograms of chemical fertilizers in an area of 1 µ. Total 350,000 to 500,000 wheat saplings and 3,000 to 4,000 maize stalks are planted in the 1 µ area. This inter-cropping has helped to increase the production of wheat by 50%. The same cropping pattern is followed along the entire irrigation district. All these measures ensure that the productivity of a specific area increases as well as water is used in an economic manner. This has enabled to attain the production level of 1 kilogram food production per cubic meter water, and the income level of farmers have increased up to 900 yuan (Indian Rupees 4,000) per head per annum.

5. <u>Water management in the Yanguan area of Zhejiang province:</u> The total area under cultivation in the project area is 1,000 hectares. The major part of the cultivable area is irrigated through lift irrigation. In spite of the rains in the range of 1300 millimeters the farmers have to face draught during the winter, the main reason for it being the irregularity of rainfall. The total numbers of villages in this area are 12 and the total population is 22,000. From the total irrigated area of 943 hectares the area under rice crop is 712 hectares. The average production of rice is 13 tons per hectare. The cash crops worth $ 1,950 per hectare are produced per year. The annual per capita income of the farmer has increased by $ 171.

Water is lifted at 28 spots in the area with the help of 32 pumps. The power consumed to operate these pumps is equal to 423 kilowatts per year. In total 76 persons (including four expert technologists from outside) are involved in the work. The entire work is managed by the people themselves and they organize the funds for the management. Only part contribution is made by the government in the running of the local irrigation infrastructure.

When we compare the land and water management in China with the one in India, the emerging picture presents a stark contrast. It seems that our policy makers and the political elite are oblivious to the terminology of scientific planning of land and water resources and the benefits that our environment could draw from the scientific use of these. Here is a case from our country which illustrates this point.

Maharashtra has fourfold cultivable land and ample water resources compared to China. At present, Maharashtra has only 16% of total cultivable land under irrigation. The proportion of irrigation from surface and one from groundwater is almost equal in the total available irrigation. Irony of the situation is that 60% of water available from large irrigation projects is spent on cultivating a single crop and that is sugarcane. Sugarcane is cultivated only on 3% of total cultivated area in the state. There are 110 sugar factories in the state[iv] at present and there is a plan to increase their number to 170 in near future. However, at present 30 factories out of the existing ones are running into losses.

At present the state government is considering investment of Rs.30,000 lakh (Rupees three billion) in the irrigation schemes and in future as well another Rs.30,000 lakh (Rupees three billion) are expected to be invested. In spite of such huge investments there is still no guarantee about the benefit of the newly created potential for irrigation to the largest number of landholders and the wider area. The total rural population in the state is 50 million and out of this population, those living under poverty line are 72% as their per capita income per annum is less than Rs.2,200. The total shareholders in the cultivable land at present are 10.8 million and their total land is 20.2 million hectares. If the available and planned water resources are distributed on the basis of the principle of social justice, then the irrigated area could be increased up to 10 million hectares (at present, the irrigated area is 3 million hectares). This would ensure landholding of 1 hectare per family living in the rural area and availability of 5,000 cubic meters of water for irrigation in a year. The recurring draughts devastate vast tracts of agricultural land due to the misuse and underutilization of irrigation. One can just imagine the colossal challenge posed to the effectiveness of our planning mechanisms by this situation.

Poverty and agricultural development[v]

Sr. No.	Factor	China	India	Maharashtra
1	Population (million)	1,238	931	84
2	Rural population	860	650	50
3	Land available per family (hectares)	0.5	1.3	1.8
4	Percent area under irrigation	50 %	35 %	16 %
5	Annual production of food grains (million tons)	480	190	14
6	Production of sugarcane (million tons)	8	15	5
7	Percent population under poverty line	7	60	60

(iv) A scheme for equitable redistribution of land and water in Maharashtra

a. Family as the unit of redistribution of land and water in Maharashtra:

To satisfy the needs of the rural population and produce surplus to be sent outside, with respect to the need of the rural producers, there is requirement of 0.2 hectares of irrigated land per head. This would require 1,000 cubic meters of water per year. This implies that

1. A family of five individuals would require 1 hectare of irrigated land and 5,000 cubic meters of water per year to obtain sufficient local employment;

2. The annual income from agriculture for this family at today's value would be Rs.30,000.

3. This level of income would be three times the current level of income indicating the line of poverty.

Nevertheless, it must be kept in mind that due to geographical conditions, it may not be possible to make the same amount of irrigated water available to all in Maharashtra. Instead, a number of studies have proved that with the help of technology and proper planning, it would be possible to provide division wise 5-8,000 cubic meters of water per farming family. Consequently, it is a necessary condition resulting out of the social obligation that agricultural production worth maximum value is obtained through each cubic meter of water available by the means of technology.

b. Organization of redistribution through the village:

The benefits of irrigation could be made available to all in the rural area of Maharashtra if 40 – 50% land under cultivation in the villages at present is provided with irrigation. The task of development of land suitable for irrigation; providing appropriate facility of water; development of various parts of the land - irrigation; and distribution of this irrigated land to all in the community on the basis of principle of equity is mainly the responsibility of the community.

With respect to the geographical conditions and planning of the available water, there would be three types of use of land in the village, namely, (a) land suitable for forest; (b) land without irrigation; and (c) land under irrigation.

c. Share in resources is optimal:

With respect to the principle of equitable distribution of water, if water and adequate land are made available to only those who are tilling the land, then it would not require to provide more than 1 hectare of irrigated land to a family of 5 and it would not be possible for the family also to cultivate land bigger than it in size with the help of limited manpower available within the family. When agriculture without irrigation is converted into one with irrigation, the manpower requirement in agriculture increases and it must be ensured that it is available throughout the year. Moreover, the family is required to live near the farm for work. This means that irrigated agriculture cannot be managed on one's own while living away from the farm.

d. Decentralization in redistribution:

According to the new arrangement emerging from the principle of redistribution of land and water, irrigation should be provided with priority to the farmers with large landholdings followed by the ones with comparatively less land and finally to the landless. However, there should not be any relaxation in the rule of 'water to the tiller' while implementing this scheme. In addition, even the family that cannot cultivate the land in spite of gaining water with priority and has to go away from the village should be allowed to retain its right over the water; and the share of water and land is reinstated to such family on its return to the original place. As well as, even the landless and those who could not cultivate land due to lack of irrigation, if they wish to come back and do agriculture, these units should be made partners in the new social contract. If we look back in the history of the problem, land and water were distributed inequitably between different social groups and agriculture largely continued without irrigation. There is little change in the situation even now. If irrigated agriculture is planned appropriately at the level of the village, and 40 – 50 % of land under cultivation is brought under irrigation then it would be possible to include all in the new arrangement. It is proved that in a diverse state like Maharashtra it is possible to do so according to various geographical areas and agro-climatic zones.

e. Redistribution and conservation:

The above step could be followed by redistribution of the land without irrigation and the forest land on the basis of the same principle and in the proportion of the redistributed irrigated land. This would offer opportunity to each family to work in all the three types of land and increase productivity in the non – irrigated and forest land as well. This would ensure conservation of the environment as well. This measure would arrest the growing erosion of land, and land will permanently remain under cover of trees.

f. Rehabilitation and the equity based arrangement:

Another major discriminatory dimension of the contemporary policy towards land and water is the mobilization of these resources for massive and rapid growth of industries in Maharashtra through major irrigation projects. Indeed, this is a national feature of the development of irrigation sector in India (World Bank and Government of India, 1997). Even though the aim of garnering support to the effort at industrialization is appreciable, there are many complex moral and serious social issues involved in such types of project. The leading ethical issue exists in the form of the very propriety of the form of change anticipated through industrialization, that is, is the form of industrialization going to be based on the felt needs of people? On the other hand, the social issue is of validity of the decision to remove the original inhabitants from the homeland and unjust treatment during the rehabilitation process.

Even though the trend of industrialization is certainly not undesirable in the light of the challenges posed by the global economic order, yet the issue of displacement and rehabilitation in the course of development of irrigation projects has persisted. There is still no proper provision for the rehabilitation of the affected families. Thus, this could become part of the new arrangement resulting from the social contract of equitable distribution of land and water.

Chapter III: Salient features of the new social policy of equitable distribution of land and water

1. Realizing the dream of Gram Swaraj

There are indications that a major shift in the focus of the policy – makers in India is occurring from exclusive economic growth to the need for evolving social mechanisms to distribute the benefits of economic growth equitably among the various sections of our society, especially so with a favorable disposition towards the poor sections of society. The shift is definitely stimulated by the constraints on the growth model in the form of the inability to distribute benefits of growth equitably.

This change in perspective has stimulated the search for alternative social mechanisms that would ensure equitable distribution of resources and their utilization in a sustainable manner[vi]. Thus, the renewed interest in the Gram Swaraj concept which is a proposed social arrangement aiming at building an egalitarian social order as well as achieving that goal through conservation of natural resources. The concept of 'Gram Swaraj' is realizable on the basis of certain principles such as (a) integrated consideration of land, water and manpower, (b) taking social and economic justice as the basis of policies related to the three elements mentioned here, (c) and vesting the responsibility of planning and management of water resources with the people at the level of the village. This calls for a major effort to re-examine the capability of our institutions at the village level to organize self-governance. The detailed facets of the problem have been discussed in the appendix 1.

2. Tenets of the new social policy of equitable distribution of land and water

However, there has been no consistent thinking about the relevance of developing watershed at the village level, and whenever required, supporting these with large irrigation projects and canal systems. The principle that 'even the landless have a right over water', and instead of the principle of 'land to the tiller' a more radical principle of 'equal water to the tiller' is necessary has not been accepted as a tenet of governance by the policy makers and politicians in our country. Indeed, these principles could prepare the foundations of a policy of redistribution of land and water resources and social integration.

In order to achieve this, there is need for abolishing private ownership of land and water in the village and create collective ownership of these resources. The regulated access to these resources would be restricted to those engaged in cultivation, an activity which would be carried out by the community for its own members. This measure would inhale life in the new social organization based on the 'social contract of redistribution'. The tenets of the new social contract of redistribution would be as follows.

(i) Integrated use of land and water;

(ii) Complete return on payment to the labor;

(iii) Labor is not required to work on land of others or seek employment elsewhere for livelihood; and instead subsists on the means made available through the guaranteed access to land and water;

(iv) The above discussed principles would form the basis of economic prosperity, conservation of environment and social solidarity. All political parties need to consider the new social policy of use of land and water. Otherwise, the expenditure on government programs would keep increasing without returns and an increasing part of rural population would be deprived of benefits of economic development and it would all continue under the name of the welfare state. Consequently, the economically weakened rural population is not able to take advantage of education, health and other facilities. This is a state of colossal loss as there are major expenditures without returns. Therefore, this pattern keeps nurturing the massive bureaucracy engaged in various sectors at the cost of the poor.

3. Integrating the social science analysis in the new social policy

Above discussion makes it sufficiently clear that we, keeping in with the alternative approach to development, look towards the village as the basis of sustainable development. This raises a question of practical nature, that is, does the contemporary Indian village in reality qualify to be the basis of an egalitarian process? The question could be modified to ask with respect to the problem of institutional set up for the new social arrangement 'whether the many traditional, local institutions associated with the governance of the village could become the instruments of change towards equitable distribution of resources essential to satisfy the basic needs of our population?'

In the contemporary village set up, there have been unequal distributions of land and water resources. Though some resources were maintained as the common property of the village, still the access to these resources would be influenced by the interests of the dominant sections of the village. Moreover, the landed gentry and other dominant groups have influence over the consumption of the produces and services from these resources. In the light of this, one could not blindly profess a delegation of authority to local institutions, especially in situations where these have been used as the means of oppression of the lower sections of the community. Therefore, undoubtedly this calls for a re-examination of the ownership and utilization patterns of resources in the Indian village. As an implication, it also calls for a critical assessment of the indigenous institutions to deliver goods on an equitable basis. This calls for a better sociological understanding about the nature of the Indian village. This understanding may perhaps help us in determining the operational limits on the choice of the village as the basis of an egalitarian social arrangement. A detailed discussion in this respect follows in Note 2.

Chapter IV: Directions of the "alternative development policy"

1. The emergent alternative development policy

The above discussion with respect to the management of water and land in a sustainable and equitable manner has illustrated the fallacious thinking about development as well as it has also highlighted the operational constraints of the policies and strategies based on the conventional perspective of development. This situation calls for new alternatives in development thinking, which is of course a process already going on in the country. However, this discussion is too broad in scope and lacks an internal coherency as the ideas reflecting on the present state of our society and the urge for newer approaches are coming from different quarters of society. The need of the hour is to consolidate our thoughts and actions in a common – though a broad and flexible – framework. The framework would be made up of not only common philosophical premises but policy outline and operational guidelines related to it. Therefore, the challenge in front of the community of policy – makers and development agencies in near future is to put heads together to set a common agenda. This would require them to go beyond their 'ethnic identities' which are rooted in their specific development experiences. The task also calls for evolving a new policy approach combining the best of the historical and functional approaches to the study of society.

2. Need for undoing the ideological and operational constraints of the established patterns

There are four major ideological and operational corner stones of the established policy making in the country which need to be undone if one has to move farther in the direction of defining the outline of a new development policy. The undoing will have to be done for certain ideological reasons but that is not a sufficient reason to do so. It is also necessary to do so in order to overcome the visible constraints on the established development practices.

(i) Growth driven economy: The problem of the growth driven economy is not merely rooted in the context of the global economic system. What guided the decisions of the policy makers in the formative stages of Indian development policy were anxieties that were politically stimulated than an objective assessment of the capability of our society to pilot new directions of social and economic experiments. Thus was born the rhetoric of 'national plan' which advocated a mix of private enterprise and controlled economy. What lied below the rhetoric was a craving for attaining high economic growth at the cost of the need for lessening the economic and social disparities. This thinking is very much drenched in the policy and plans of the country aimed at industrialization as the priority and have relegated agriculture to the secondary position. Therefore, one finds a de-emphasizing of the land reforms instituted in the States throughout the period of the first three five – year plans. In the scheme of development as envisaged in these plans, agriculture was looked upon as a 'bargain sector' which could supplement cheap food and raw material to the growing industrial sector. There was never serious attempt to change the agrarian economic and social structure lest the growth instinct of the rich peasantry was not killed. Another incentive to the growth instinct of the rich peasantry came in the form of the expansion of irrigation and input supply of credit, chemicals and fertilizers - particularly, during the period called as Green Revolution. Again as it happened in case of land, these resources were also monopolized by the rich peasantry.

This process directly culminated in the present condition of unequal distribution of land and water resources. Indeed the unequal distribution of land, water and other important agricultural resources has reached such alarming proportions that the very economic and social fabric of Indian society is threatened to be torn apart. This risk stands very high chances of materialization as the entire issue has attained political overtones and it bursts out in a wide range of conflicts throughout the country. Though the outbursts are apparently unrelated with each other and the protagonists in these situations concentrate on specific issues like prices for agriculture produces, environmental crises centering on irrigation projects, or redistribution of land and water resources; yet the roots of all these problems could be traced down to the problem of disorganized distribution and utilization patterns of natural resources, the bottom of which is underlined by the issue of equitable distribution and proper utilization of land and water resources.

(ii) Macro perspective of development: The pioneers of planning in India subordinated all facts about our social and economic life to the perceived need for accumulation of seed capital. Therefore, the focus was more on adoption and maximum application of modern technology for reaping maximum economic growth than carefully sifting of the facts related to the conditions and problems emerging at the regional level. This approach definitely reaped bounty in the form of development of large industrial infrastructure, cash incentives and mechanized agriculture initially; but as the country advances more and more into the future, these very gains seem to play the role of constraints on the growth of our economy as well as foster the de-motivating factors for the overwhelmingly large section of the population. Therefore, lately there is an increasing demand for decentralization of the planning mechanisms and creation of institutions to suit the regional needs of development from various quarters of society. There are many issues involved in the process of transition from a macro perspective of development to the decentralized one. These issues are of course both of an ideological as well as an operational nature and are closely linked with each other. These have been discussed in detail in appendix 'issues of participation of people in development management'.

(iii) Centralized governance: The gaining of independence also witnessed consolidation of the State in the country. This was thought as a necessary measure for bringing about the required changes in the economic structure and holding down any discontent that could upset the economic agenda of the newly independent nation. The anxiety of the political elite was reflected on many occasions - a class which was virtually an *infantile* class of policy – makers that regarded any movements from any part of society that smelt of a call (even when concealed) for decentralization with suspicion. Thus, the political concerns related to over - empowering of the State as well as the economic agenda went hand in hand and provided impetus to each other. Only recently that the Indian polity has started showing sensitivity towards the issue of decentralization (the findings of the Task Force of the Planning Commission of India are briefly presented in Note 3). Nevertheless, before parting with this point for other ones, it may be submitted that centralized governance is (with its inherent complexities) as much a product as it is an instrument of governance. This dimension of the issue always needs to be kept in mind while discussing the issue as no human society could ever think of achieving a form of governance according to a blue print.

(iv) Sector based approach to planning: The model of development adopted by India harbors the sectoral approach to planning. These sectors have been defined with respect to the theory of capital accumulation. Therefore, the relationship between two or more sectors of economy is defined with respect to the various indices associated with the flow of capital within single sectors and between them. The effectiveness of the development plans is, thus, measured in terms of the capital generated by a particular sector and its contribution to the cumulative economic growth of the economic system. However, the economic model of development, especially one harnessed to the larger than life goal of achieving economic growth at the cost of equality in distribution have failed to achieve development without any 'lags'.

Therefore, still even after forty five years of planning, we find disparities in the performance of the various sectors of our economy which inevitably leads to dragging of feet by different sectors ultimately resulting into slowing of the pace of economic growth. Another major limitation of the planning in the country with grave implications was the lack of attention to the consequences of various programs on the process of redistribution of benefits within the population. Hitherto, the policy makers and political elite have managed to go unscathed in spite of ignoring the issues related to equity involved in development planning and implementation. Therefore, what we have in our society after fifty years of independence is often in the form of polarities in various spheres of life.

These polarities have led to serious social tensions in our society which are frequently exploding in the form of political and communal crises. The first six to seven plans (five year plans) of the country assumed that if there is 'sufficient' structural balance between the sector of capital goods and agriculture, there would be a definite trend of trickle down of economic growth from the higher strata to the lower ones. This simply did not happen. These limitations on the traditional model of development call for drastic changes in our approach and methodology of development.

Therefore, now is the need for substitution of the sectoral strategies of development planning with an operational scheme that is sensitive to the regional patterns of resource mobilization and utilization, local social and economic conditions, and having an integrated approach to development. This would also require us to move away from the economic policy based on the premises of primacy of capital accumulation in favor of equitable distribution of growth. The last point is crucial for the effectiveness of the decision to move away from the sectoral strategies of planning as these are essentially based on a 'narrow' perception of human life. If our society has to move in the direction of a more humane state of existence, then that would require us to change our idea of development too. The ideal of a development that fragments the life of the people and an individual is not tenable with the ideals of a harmonious civic society envisaged from time to time by social visionaries.

3. Outline of an alternative development policy

A. Ideological premises

The alternative development policy would bear certain salient features such as

(a) It will be holistic in perspective

(b) It will employ the historical - analytical methodology for exploring the nature of the contemporary problems

(c) It will rely on the concept of quality of life as not merely an ideal but also as an index of development

(d) It will underpin the integrated nature of the different dimensions of human life, therefore, providing the conceptual framework for integrated planning of development programs under different conventional sectors of planning (in this respect it might be said to be closely related with the post-modernist approach and perhaps tracking down the ancestry to the indigenous ideologies of India)

(e) It would emphasize the importance of people themselves as the organizational basis of the efforts of planning

(f) It would select the local forms of mobilizing people as the strategy for implementing development programs.

With respect to these salient features the ideological premises of the alternative policy would be

(i) Plurality of cultures and ideals is the basis for development; nevertheless, convergence or at least exchange between different trends in society is essential

(ii) Sustainability of development is dependent on the sustainability of the environment and the compatibility between the change implicit in a development program with the culture of the people

(iii) There would be a drastic shift in the role of the state from one of the 'omnipotent hand' to a 'partner in development'

(iv) There is a mutual relationship between the processes of construction and deconstruction

(v) Subjection of all forms of knowledge (this refers to the dichotomous categories of scientific knowledge and technology based on it, and the indigenous knowledge) to evaluation based on common ideological values

(vi) Primacy of the capacity of production over the principle of production

(vii) In contrast to the conventional view, it is human needs that should determine the technology which in turn should determine the market

(viii) Indiscriminate consumerism replaces creative production

(ix) Science and technology should be dissociated from any form of exploitation

(x) Establishing the principles of ecological communities as the guidelines for the anticipated new institution building process

(xi) Equity is the core of all social exchanges

B. State as one of the partners in development

It has been observed that the state has consistently concentrated power unto itself in independent India. This has been paralleled by a decrease in the power and autonomy enjoyed by various social groups. Thus, the relationship between the state power and people's involvement in decision – making has been inversely proportional. Therefore, the Indian society has reached a stage when it cannot dispense with the State as the major catalyst of change and at the same time needs to curtail the excessive concentration of powers in it. This paradox has a close bearing on the problem of the relationship between the State and the other constituted entities of people.

The intensity of the issue is highlighted in the light of the fact that in the traditional Indian social structure various social groups enjoyed high degree of autonomy. The process of decrease in the autonomy hastened up during the colonial rule and was continued even after independence. Meanwhile, there emerged other major forces besides the State which represented the aspirations and interests of various sections of the people. These forces emerged as obviously the State was not able to accommodate the conflicting interests and aspirations of various sections. The existence of these forces like the voluntary organizations renders a balance to the power equilibrium between the State and the people. Nevertheless, the relationship between these forces and the State are yet to be streamlined within the constitutional frame of Indian State. Moreover, this streamlining must be of a 'constructive' nature wherein all the actors work towards resolution of problems through 'non-violent' means.

The process of operationalization of the constructive partnership between the State and other forces would be smooth and productive when convincing solutions to the following two interrelated questions are provided through consensus. The first among the two is of a generic nature which tries to encompass a broad range of processes, while the second one is more specific focusing on the potential of voluntary organizations to arbitrate on behalf of people.

(i) How to induce changes in the policy making processes of the State?

There are two major dimensions to the discussion related to this question, viz. (a) the involvement of people in the executive functions of the State; and (b) relationship of the State vis-à-vis other potential forces in society.

The answer to this question ought to be provided with reference to the position that 'people can realize their own development'. This approach implies that people should have a direct control over decision making related to their own development. How best would this be achieved without effecting changes in the setup of political executive and monitoring of the role of the bureaucracy by the people themselves?

The 'other forces' include the ones which have a formalized structure as well as those which have a phenomenal existence but do not have an internally coordinated existence like in case of the forces with a formalized structure. In the context of the alternative policy of development, the forces with formalized structure especially refer to the political parties and organizations, the corporate industrial organizations, the membership organizations like the farmers' unions or the farm workers' union that negotiate the interests of the specific classes in society, and the voluntary organizations. The phenomenal forces mainly include the market and the social entities with a corporate constitution that have formed the backbone of the social organization of our society for at least a few centuries like the village and the social institutions associated with it, as well as, traditional occupational associations that have a constitutional existence.

The question at stake here is not one of merely defining the relationship of the State with each of these separately; on the other hand, it is one of creating a grid of power relations and conditions conducive for the operation of such a grid. This would require induction of major legal provisions in our executive systems on the one hand and on the other hand, a direct involvement of these various entities in the defining of policies of the State on an equal footing. This would certainly not take place if we continue with the present political-judicial systems without any change in their mandate and prerogatives within the ambit of the country's constitution. In near future, there is need for closer working between these entities in order to attain a decentralized but coherent and dynamic system of execution. Therefore, there is need for assessing the efficacy of the Panchayati Raj system that is still being introduced in the various states of the country. As well as, it calls for an assessment of the sector wise performance of the decision making mechanisms and explore the scope for inclusion of one or all of the entities described above in the decision making and implementation of plans.

(ii) Relationship of Voluntary Organizations with bureaucracy

It is in the light of the last point mentioned above regarding the possibility of involvement of VOs in the decision-making process that one needs to explore the scope for closer relationship between Voluntary Organizations and the State for policy making. The relationship between the two has always been one of conflicting and competition mainly since the country won independence. However, with the changing context of the working of the

Voluntary Organizations, many of them grew close to political elite (which is synonymous to the State in Indian context), which ultimately resulted in some of them becoming instrument of the State. One has to devise the operational process of cooperation in execution carefully as the Voluntary Organizations have often been accused of either falling in line with the government positions or becoming substitutes to government institutions in planning and allocation of development resources.

C. Do voluntary organizations form a force that can play a role in policy-making

The history of the relationship between the State and the Voluntary Organizations in India has been a checkered one. Sometimes, they have stood as contenders in face of each other and some other times, the state has succeeded in co-opting the Voluntary Organizations in accomplishing its objectives. However, in spite of the occasional cooperation between the State and the VOs, there has never been a consistent and productive cooperation between the two. There are multiple factors which have created this condition. These are the ones which need to be seriously considered by both the State as well as the Voluntary Organizations in order to play a complementary role in the mission of changing the Indian society towards better conditions of existence.

- Accepting the importance of the State as the most critical factor in social change thus, making it a potential change catalyst for a better social system by the Voluntary Organizations. This needs to be reciprocated by an acceptance of the capacity of other constituted entities to enforce desirable decisions by the State

- Voluntary Organizations in India have been absorbed into the particulars of their independent workings and therefore, they are unable to consolidate their lessons into a commonly intelligible format

An analogous phenomenon is that the voluntary sector is a divided house where the interests and specific aims of Voluntary Organizations become the barriers between them. Presently, the Voluntary Organizations are divided into four major categories on basis of distinct approaches followed by them, namely, poverty alleviation; natural resources management; educational and the welfare approach. There is nothing wrong with these approaches as such. The fault lies with the over - allegiance of the Voluntary Organizations with their respective approaches. The entrenched adherence to their own approach has blinded them to the limitations of their own programs and the strengths of other approaches. This is a major block in the elevation of the

Voluntary Organizations to a level where their recommendations could be incorporated in policies.

- Research and development has always been a weak aspect of the working of Voluntary Organizations. This proves a major hindrance in the transformation of the valuable experience of the Voluntary Organizations into policies.

- The 'contacts' between the two have most of the time been one at the superficial level, and both sides have shown reluctance to understand each other's problems and positions. This has reflected in the communication pattern between the two. It has always been characterized by forging of vertical linkages between the two (usually with the bureaucracy above and the Voluntary Organizations below). There have been hardly any systematic efforts to establish functional linkages between the two (based on practical assessment of reality) horizontally. If this frame of network is evolved in the country in near future through systematic program, it would substantiate the decentralization of decision making and implementation with respect to various facets of the development of population in different parts of the country.

D. Water/Land redistribution as the crucial factors in sustainable development

From the discussion in the earlier parts of the book, it is apparent that agriculture was never considered a priority sector by the Indian planners. Therefore, the majority of our population which depended on agriculture for livelihood was deprived of the opportunity for gainful employment and a better quality of life on par with the other sections of population. The consequences of such an attitude of indifference were not restricted to lack of sufficient opportunities for employment. Another major consequence of this attitude was that the rural population was handicapped with respect to the capability to innovate new avenues for livelihood. This set off a process which ultimately resulted in the pushing of majority population in the rural area below poverty line, which ultimately forms a large part of the total population.

This is demonstrated definitely none other than the fact that our policies and approach towards land reforms never have been implemented in a wholehearted manner. There has never been serious thought spared for the equitable distribution and proper utilization of agricultural inputs like irrigation and other material and manpower inputs. The consequences of this lack of determination to improve agriculture to its productive best are very much visible for everyone to see. On the other hand, our policy makers always preferred a myopic view of the development problems. Therefore, they could never see the point that the improvement of agriculture sector is very much a social problem than a problem of technology. They could never see the point that our average farmer had been exposed to peculiar forms of social and economic exploitation consistently over a period of almost hundred and fifty years before independence. This had weakened his capability as a producer and ruined the economic, ecological and social viability of the farm on which he worked.

The conditions pertaining to availability of land and water differ drastically from one region to another in the country, yet there could be a few common elements in the water and land related policies of the central government and the various state governments. These are briefly presented in the following section on 'the elements of the social policy of land and water distribution as the basis of an alternative development policy'. Moreover, the significance of these elements should be understood in the light of the concept of sustainable development which emphasizes the cyclical relationship between water, land, manpower and the social systems of man. The relationship operates on the basis of the fundamental principle that 'the interaction between man and nature is mediated through society, therefore, more integrated and harmonious the organization of human society, it increases the potential for a creative and harmonious relationship between man and nature'.

E. Elements of the social policy as the basis of alternative development policy

- Change in policy: The permanent link between sustainable development and water can be established only after a major change in the fundamental policy of the State towards water management. This calls for a better coordination between the agencies (the government as well as non - government ones) involved in the management of water resources. Existence of these agencies at present is superficially functional and they mostly enjoy a vertical relationship without any serious contact among themselves. Another requirement in this respect would be a radical change in the attitude of the policy makers towards the use of water. To be little more specific, it calls for a shift from the established single - track approach to the problem. The legislation related to land resources must cover water resources.

- People's participation: The problem of water scarcity in the semi-arid environment needs to be solved through conservation of water resources and their management with respect to the complexities, variety and prevalent instability in such regions. This should be the foundation of the practice of sustainable development. However, experience from different regions has shown that people in the water-scare environments have already evolved techniques and mechanisms that ensure conservation and proper utilization of water. Indeed these are part of the indigenous knowledge of people which have been overlooked by the policy makers. Moreover, these age-old systems have helped to increase the productivity of land.

This dimension calls for management of the resources for sustainable development under the control of the local people. This is definitely a challenge to the imaginative thinking of the policy makers and the non-government agencies. Indeed a burden to the responsibility of non-government agencies is added in the sense that they have to work as liaison between government and people. They should particularly ensure control of the local people over the decision making processes.

- Optimal use of the irrigation: The physical expansion of irrigation and management of the facilities should be directly subordinated to the goal of generating adequate employment in the rural areas. Indeed, this is likely to arrest the massive migration that takes place between different parts of the country.

- Integrated management: Modernization is engulfing our society from all the sides, which is fraught with many risks of breakdown of the fundamental social systems. This is mainly happening since we have not been looking into the interdependence of the various systems. This calls for establishment of mechanisms that would allow integrated planning of education, production systems, political control mechanisms and social institutions. This description of a desirable situation has to be understood as a potential direction towards which our society could strive. The measures implicit in the direction can be very specific such as

(i) Incorporating the lessons learnt through the social experiments of the Voluntary Organizations and individuals in the development policies

(ii) Turning the direction of the existing 'development' programs from permanent dependence of people on bureaucracy and market systems to self-reliance which necessitates conservation and proper management of local natural resources

(iii) Resources are squandered in implementing unproductive programs in the rural areas. This fragmented approach to development must be substituted by a more constructive and integrated one. This might include investment of large capital in creating 'security of water' for the rural people. This would be possible if the resources inadequately vested in different schemes and programs of the government are diverted towards a common program aiming to create this security. This also calls for a closer work between the government, the voluntary organizations and individuals. There is a need for enacting laws and rules based on them that would ensure a planning for sustainable development in a decentralized manner. Indeed, judicious distribution of water resources should be the core of a drive in this direction.

- Land and water management as the basis of tribal development: Tribal groups form a major portion of the country's population. Their percentage in the total population changes from one state to another. Even within the state this proportion differs drastically from one part to another. Nevertheless, except perhaps a few instances in the north-eastern parts of the country, the tribal groups are milling under the burden of poverty. This poverty though apparently imposed by natural conditions in reality is a product of the attitude of indifference among the political elite towards their plight. If the aim of poverty alleviation among the tribal populations has to be realized seriously, then there must be a concentration on the improvement of the habitat of the tribes. For example, there should be a radical program of change in the lives of the tribes inhabiting hilly rain-fed areas. The tribal people in these areas are encroaching on the marginal dry lands and forest as they do not have access to irrigation. The situation can be alleviated through

(i) Providing irrigation on a sizable portion of the land under cultivation in the tribal areas

(ii) Redistribution of land on the basis of equity in tribal villages and creation of collective ownership of the irrigation resources at the village level.

- Lessons of Pani Panchayat movement: The experiment of Pani Panchayat in Purandhar Tehsil of Pune district has proved the viability of the watershed based planning of land, water and manpower. The principles that emerged from the experiment are

(i) Water would not be provided in proportion to the size of the population. On the contrary, it would be provided in proportion of the unit of 0.5 acre per head in a family up to a limit of 1,000 cubic meters.

(ii) Changing the cropping patterns in such a manner that the crops that require a cultivation period equal to the entire year are dropped permanently. Only seasonal crops with respect to the availability of water are cultivated. Indeed, water is made available to crops requiring a period of eight months at most.

(iii) Even the landless would have access to the water made available through watershed.

(iv) Divesting the water rights from the land rights, thus, instituting collective ownership of water resources. Therefore, 'water to the tiller' like 'land to the tiller' could become the basis of a progressive policy. Indeed, land can be transacted but not water.

(v) The community contributes 20 % of the seed capital required for the starting of the project.

These five principles are indeed the learning points to those regions of the country which have been reeling under similar economic and agro-ecological conditions (which in fact would cover large tracts of the country).

Note 1

The dilemma of a revolution

The World Bank and Government of India have observed that Irrigation is a crucial factor for agricultural production in a monsoon – dependent farming system, as well as, basic economic infrastructure facilitating inter-sectoral economic linkages both within and across regions. Indeed, at the national and regional levels, agricultural growth in particular and rural development in general has closely followed expansion of irrigation. It is asserted that irrigation has contributed tremendously to maturation of the Green Revolution in the country. The food grain production has gone up from 50 million tons in 1947 to 196 million tons at present in India. Even though the population increased two and half times more than what it was at the time of independence; nevertheless, not only we have managed to become self-reliant with respect to food grain and other agricultural products, we are even exporting these items. The main reason for this was that irrigation was coupled with agricultural development. Indeed this substantial growth could not have been possible without development of irrigation.

However, the euphoria over the Green Revolution has died out and there is a mood of introspection among the policy makers. The impact of the 'miracle' of the Green Revolution needs to be understood in two separate but closely linked contexts, namely, the increased disparities at the national and regional level – and even at the level of areas smaller than regions with respect to agricultural production, and the contribution of the changes intrinsic to the Green Revolution to economic inequalities. The most conspicuous malady of it has been that Green Revolution is not spread out evenly in different regions and sub-regions of the country. It is concentrated specifically in areas where irrigation is available in abundance.

Note 2

Is the community a fiction?

The Indian village has always been projected as a homogenous entity embodying all the virtues of an 'egalitarian community'. There are two major factors that have helped boosting such a perspective about the Indian village, viz. political dogmatism and dogmatic environmentalism. Therefore, the Indian village has often been portrayed as a repository of egalitarian ethos by the advocates of both these trends. The third important factor is historical in nature arising out of the fact that the village was retained as the lowest unit of governance by the colonial rulers, and their legacy was carried forward by the political elite of independent India.

On the other hand is the macro analytical and evolutionary perspective which looks upon the village as the part of the 'part community and part society complex'. This perspective highlights the integration of the village with the larger social system and the mechanisms that ensure autonomy of the village. It is this perspective that is more objective in its treatment of the problem of significance of the village in the social change towards an egalitarian social order. The 'part community and part society' approach has definite implications for the Indian situation. These are as follows.

i. Society is stratified into unequally located categories based on principles of economic status and social status separately. Nevertheless, there are mechanisms that connect the economic stratification with the social stratification. Indeed, in the Indian context, there is an antithetical relationship between the social status and economic roles concomitant with an economic category.

ii. In the Indian context, the stratification is dominated by the prescriptive norms and ideas than the ascriptive ones which harbor individualism and class system based on one's ability to control the means of production. The prescriptive Indian system has consisted of ossified class relations which are so because of the undifferentiated nature of different aspects of life.

iii. The village is a composite settlement constituted by groups based on the mode of extended family. These groups have a specific economic relationship with the other co-habiting groups. This economic relationship is defined by the functions required to be performed on the farms.

iv. Indian village also carries a communal identity as the village also strives to attain commonly defined goals. These goals are mainly guided by the economic requirements related with the local farming systems. This communal identity is 'negotiable' as members of the village negotiate their social prestige and economic assets with other social entities.

v. In the course of negotiation of its social prestige and economic interests every village needs to define its own identity. This further requires defining the boundaries of the community. The definition is enforced based on cultural peculiarities and geographical landmarks. This definition is enforced through explicit as well as implicit patterns of use of the ecosystem in which the village is located.

Note 3

A paradox: the rise of State Power and decline of People's Power

The disadvantages and limitations of the excessively centralized governance are best documented by a Task Force of the Planning Commission of India.

- *Alienation of people and their power*
- *Failure of the development system to deliver services to people*
- *Failure of the system to deliver social justice*
- *Subordination of the local representative bodies to the bureaucracy*
- *Risks implicit in the Panchayati Raj bill*
- *The executive estate – power without responsibility*
- *Nexus between the political and bureaucratic powers*
- *Quality through self - management vs. inefficiency of the bureaucracy*
- *Attitude to regulate and control than catalyze*
- *The anti-sustainability stance of the State*
- *Fragmentation of polity through electioneering*

Appendix 1

1. Relevance of indigenous Institutions for Decentralized Planning

The features of the Indian village discussed in Note 2 have a direct bearing on the problem of creating institutional setup for governance of development at the level of villages. Lately the decentralized perspective of development emphasizes the primacy of the community as the basic unit of planning. However, there are many views among academicians and policy makers regarding the qualification of the Indian village as the proper candidate for the definition of a community. The question involved in the debate is whether the many traditional, local institutions associated with the governance of the village could become the instruments of change towards equitable distribution of resources essential to satisfy the basic needs of our population.

In the traditional village setup there has been unequal distribution of land and water resources. Moreover, the landed gentry and other dominant groups have influence over the consumption of the produces and services from these resources. In the light of this, one could not blindly profess a delegation of authority to local institutions, especially in situations where these have been used as the means of oppression of the weaker sections of the community. Therefore, no doubt this calls for a reexamination of the patterns of ownership and utilization of resources in the Indian village. As an implication, it also calls for a critical assessment of the capability of the indigenous institutions to deliver goods on an equitable basis.

Importance of the problem is also to be understood in the light of the emerging constraints on the decentralized perspective of development. These constraints are imposed by the growing complexity of the production – market systems. The complexity is set in because of (a) the expansion of the economic domains of the modern industry business complexes on global scale which obviously brings in play a number of political and economic factors; (b) agriculture being subordinated to the profit motives than considered as the source of satisfying the basic needs of man (indeed the proposition could be extended to include the forests and other natural resources too), and (c) subversion of the need based consumption to technology driven market system (which has already become a global system).

In the light of the challenges posed by the modern economic systems (that are mainly a product of the capitalist mode of production), there are two alternatives with regard to the issue of the propriety of the village as the unit of planning, that is, either undoing the total makeup of the modern market and technology driven systems or the villages becoming the viable corporate economic bodies vibrantly responding to the changing patterns in the larger economic order. Is there a third alternative possible or necessary is a point that depends on the assessment of the two alternatives considered here. The two alternatives considered here should be assessed on the basis of their practicality and the social, economic and political implications of each in the light of the complexity of social and economic systems mentioned here. Therefore, the assessment would be done with respect to

a. The possibility of delivering social and economic goods to all in society on the basis of the principle of equity

b. Building the capability for offering productive role to all in society

c. Potential for ensuring participation of all productive sections of society in defining and deciding the alternatives of production and their utility

It may be reiterated that the desirability of a third alternative depends on the practicality and implications of the two alternatives considered here.

The merit of a third alternative would depend on its ability to overcome constraints faced by the first two alternatives. Therefore, it is important to understand the potentials and limitations as well as risks and opportunities concomitant with either of the two alternatives (the third alternative may be a blend of the two alternatives considered here. It would consist of undoing of the present market – production systems and establishing villages as the basic units of an economic organization based on equity).

The past and present development related policy of the Indian State and the changes therein should be scrutinized in the light of these alternatives (particularly, with reference to their implications). This is a pre-condition to the wider discussion on the desirability of the two approaches proposed here. The scrutiny of the past and present policies and the new alternatives though carried out with reference to the possibility of accepting the village as the unit of development planning would encompass all the broader issues involved in development planning.

2. Growth in the Mass of Landless and Small Landholders?

The Indian feudal agricultural system relied on the labor provided by the tenants and the laborers (many a time tied to the landlord through custom of bondage). This system allowed subsistence of the tenants, particularly so in the decades preceding the consolidation of the colonial power over the entire sub-continent. There was little effort wasted by the colonial rulers to abolish the interest of the feudal class, yet they definitely saw to it that the virtual sovereignty of the landlords was curtailed. This aspect has been discussed in details earlier. Now we may look into the process, how the policies of finding local allies by the colonial rulers led into the aggravation of the problem of equitable and sustainable use of water and land resources in the country.

The colonial rulers did nothing to protect the rights of the tenants between 1793 and 1856. On the other hand, the local landlords were compelled to join hands with the colonial masters in collecting maximum rent from the tenants. There were some attempts towards protecting the tenancy rights after that. But these could not stop the exploitation of the tenants in the face of the eruption of a class of intermediaries who negotiated between the landlords and farmers, and the strengthening of the interests of the landlords. A reaction to the land reforms tried by the colonial government was the removal of the tenants from land by the landlords.

Another phenomenon that facilitated the uprooting of the cultivators from land was the rapid growth in population which mounted tremendous pressure on the cultivable land. The primary effect of the rapid population growth was the shrinking of the landholdings. This rendered the small landholdings unproductive which forced farmers to leave hopes in gains from land and migrate for wage labor. Indeed this is still a major factor that has plagued the Indian agriculture. The problem has attained complexity as there is uneven distribution of population across the country and there is no regulatory system for controlling the movements of the population and no clear policy for settlement or rehabilitation of the displaced sections of rural population.

The land reforms were seriously tried out in different states after independence (it is a concurrent subject). The sincerity of doing so, the seriousness of goal and the readiness of government machinery to implement the legislation related to land reform of course differed from one state to another. Therefore, the nature of the problem of landless and small farmers has become extremely complex in the post – independence period.

In some states, the feudal class with its traditional influence has been either completely routed out or diminished to inconsequential size. This change has been accompanied by the emergence of the class of self – cultivators from among the erstwhile mass of tenants. The mass of the self-cultivating farmers consists of two divisions, namely the rich farmers and the marginal and small farmers. The rich farmers have benefited most from the devolution of the land rights, the public sector infrastructure created for inputs in the agriculture sector, and the systems created for ensuring a successful green revolution. These factors coupled with an enterprising approach and availability of labor has enabled the direct land-tillers to reap good benefits from agriculture. In some places, even one could find the ex-landlords having transformed themselves into direct land-tillers. Thus, the emergence of the class of land-tillers also denotes the phenomenon of emboldening of the capitalist element in the agriculture of the country. The creation of the new market systems is rather forcing the defunct feudal pockets to disappear. This has indeed become the irreversible trend in Indian agriculture.

However, the emergence of the class of capitalist farmers and the consolidating of the capital oriented market system has also seen the pushing of an increasingly large mass of landholders and marginal farmers towards the margins of the agricultural economy. This marginalization is economic, political as well as social in nature. The small and marginal farmers find it increasingly difficult to sustain farming as a profitable enterprise on the small landholdings. They are pushed aside in the competition for the limited resources made available by the public sector, by the rich farmers and they are unable to benefit from any political decisions that would protect their farms, rights and provide them entrepreneurial opportunities as they are largely a disorganized class. Indeed, they have grievances common with the landless agricultural laborers than with their so-called brotherhood of rich farmers as the ranks of laborers are obviously filled up by the small and marginal farmers and they are also exposed to the same economic and social risks as the completely disempowered laborers.

3. Need for integrated regional planning of water resources

In Maharashtra state eighty percent rainfall is dependent on southwest Indian monsoon and the rest on the rain clouds coming from the Bay of Bengal. From the total precipitation, about 30% is available through surface and percolated water. The meteorological studies of the twentieth century have proved that the average patterns of precipitation has remained the same for a period of 74 years; while the remaining 26 years are made up of half the period with rains 10% below of the average and the other half 10% above the average. It is sufficient to meet all water related needs of the state. In spite of this favorable condition, it is grudgingly complained that agriculture production in the state is not stable as it is dependent on the 'unpredictable' monsoon. It is a perpetual picture that parts of the region suffer from famines due to over – precipitation and other parts suffer from famines due to less than average precipitation simultaneously. To top all this, majority of the irrigation available is given for cultivating sugarcane. Therefore, the state still has to import the food grains. In addition to this, extensive degradation of the land under sugarcane cultivation has been observed. What has happened in Maharashtra is more or less representative of the fate of agriculture in other states of the country. These are all indicators of the exploitative mode of operation and lack of a pro – people approach to agriculture development. This problem would have been solved if agriculture is not left completely at the mercy of the rains; and on the contrary, coordination in the storage and conservation of the rainwater and its distribution as well as use is ensured.

This calls for plans spanning over a long period and presence of foresight among the policy-makers. Otherwise the situation will persist forever till the agriculture reaches the brink of collapse.

4. Failures of economic paradigm of development

The patterns of development in the country in the initial three decades also highlighted certain dilemmas of development process, which had to be solved to stabilize the development process.

These dilemmas are as following –

1. Development vs Non – development

2. Indigenous vs Exogenous development

3. Self – reliance vs Interdependence

4. Growth vs Distribution

5. Centralized Planning vs Decentralized Planning

6. Development vs Environment

7. Physical Investment vs Investment in Human Capital

The exclusive faith in economic indicators of development was primarily based on the premise that 'monetary and physical benefits of economic growth would percolate down from higher strata to lower ones of society'. These premises were indeed not entirely unfounded as economic processes in the industrial nations of the west in the later parts of the nineteenth century and early part of the twentieth century had shown a labor oriented growth in employment, subsequently followed by improvement in living conditions (Chakravarty, 1987).

The over – emphasis by developing countries on economic indicators of development is pointed out in many documents like the Impact of Development Strategies on the Rural Poor Report (1988) states that "1. Most developing countries continue to allocate a smaller share of public expenditure to agriculture than their share of income from agriculture...2. Between 1975 and 1979 and between 1980 and 1984, a majority of developing countries increased the allocation of public expenditure to agriculture relative to the share of agriculture to Gross Domestic Product, although the ratio continued to be disproportionately low in many countries..."

This faith in economic development was reflected in the programs of many countries including India. This is expressed in following description of the scene in the report of the Food and Agriculture Organization conference in Agrarian Reform and Development (1988), "...many development plans...have incorporated explicit targets for employment and growth, while others incorporate some antipoverty policies, which include: (a) asset distribution; (b) asset or skill development of the poor; (c) employment generation...the Indian seventh five – year plan (1985 – 1990) contains a programmatic approach towards poverty alleviation, with specific targets for the reduction of number of people below the poverty line from the 37% in 1985 to 26% in 1990..."

The same picture existed on the Indian scene also for a considerably long period with the policy makers' main focus on the economic targets. This is very much evident in the historical fact that the Mahalanobis Model adopted by the Indian rulers in the early 1950s put thrust on economic growth. This observation is substantiated by Narain (1982). While taking an overview of the changing development perspective, particularly in India, he ascertains that initially Indian model of development was indeed influenced by an economic perspective. This inference is supported by Dube too (1983). He is discussing the fallacy of the doctrine of economic development as the major goal that is substantiated by the Indian experience. He points out that, "...it is evident that totally growth - oriented approach to development is not possible in the developing countries..."

According to the same author, "this faith in economic growth was reinforced in the minds of the planners in India because of certain structural loopholes in the economic infrastructure of the newly independent State such as acute deficiency of material capital, low speed of capital accumulation, less than threshold availability of employment, low rates of conversion of savings into productive investment, a marginally existent industrial sector to accommodate surplus labor from agriculture etc. Consequently, policy - makers and planners in India for the majority of five – year plans focused on creation and maintenance of large – sized infrastructure; development of heavy industries; modernization of agriculture etc."

It is apparent that nations in different parts of the world tended to over – emphasize the economic goals of development than having a comprehensive view of development including the social goals. For instance, it is discussed in details by Gunnar Myrdal (1968) that "with the consolidation of the modern nation – states in the industrial revolution, rulers in the west as well as in other quarters of the world put exclusive emphasis on the economic indicators of development. Indeed, this approach had its own set of repercussions too. This is especially true in the case of the countries of South Asia; thus, the need to de-emphasize the exclusive importance of the economic targets of development."

The regional report of land reforms in the late 1960s and throughout the 1970s in different developing countries as presented in the same document point out that "invariably the land reforms carried out half-heartedly in many countries have led to a growth of either capital farming by landlords or the rise of middle class of farmers who have ushered in the era of Green Revolution."

These conditions have largely to do with the sectorial planning practices in India which look upon human life as a segmented entity. In such a situation, links mostly exist in an indirect manner vertically between specialized programs at the bottom and the decision – makers at the top. No horizontal links are conceived between different dimensions of the life conditions of the population. Similarly, no decisive links are conceived among the beneficiaries of different development programs at the grassroots level. These factors cumulatively lead to alienation of masses from the mainstream of development processes. This situation has led to a dependence of large sections of population on government and other centrally operating agencies to satisfy even their basic needs. This has resulted in lack of compatibility between resource inputs and outputs.

If this situation has to be remedied, inter – linking at two levels is necessary, namely, (i) policy level link between different dimensions of quality of population on the one hand, and (ii) between quality of population and physical resources investment on the other. This would help systematically measure and correlate changes in widely separated spheres of social life. Incorporation of cultural constraints in development planning could be another policy level relevant provision.

5. Primacy of the issue of equity in land/water distribution in the light of this failure

(i) The above discussion has proved that there is a close link between the emphasis on the economic growth (without ensuring distribution of economic benefits of it to the wider sections of society) and the non – committal attitude of Indian political elite towards equitable distribution of the land and water resources. The present form of economic growth could be aptly described as the extravagance of the top strata of Indian polity. Indeed this is an outcome of the combination of empty egalitarian rhetoric with the implicit policy of encouraging the exclusive social and economic interest of the elites consisting of the urban based industrial - business class, middle class, bureaucrats, politicians, feudal landlords and the new class of the middle class farmers (Dandekar, 1980).

(ii) The state of affluence and accretion of benefits by the elite is based on the links between the policy of development and the systems adopted for governance. These are

• The universally shared model of modernization along the lines of western countries by all elite sections of our society provides an impetus to the perspective based on economic growth

• Monopolization of the resources for development by the elite sections through political domination

• Loopholes in the development infrastructure which enables usurpation of benefits targeted at the poor by the elite sections

• Rationalization of the inability to bring about a radical transformation in society in the form of the Nehruvian doctrine of National Plan which advocated the convergence of two practically incompatible choices, that is, the concentration of production by itself in selected and favorable areas; and to develop the backward areas at the same time

• Achieving economic growth without creating the mechanisms for equitable distribution of benefits of it

• Insensitivity to the linkages between the various sectors of development which has proved dearly to the structure of the development policies and plans in our country

• Growth model dominated the agriculture planning from the beginning of the five-year plan system. Therefore, consequently the emphasis was led on the commercial agriculture which is dependent on intense irrigation, high chemical inputs, and production of crops with commercial value than food grains capable of satisfying the nutritional needs of the entire population in an economic manner. This strategy helped to grow the agricultural production manifold in a span of approximately two and half decades; yet it also subverted the relationship between the agricultural production and market; that is, the operative forces of the market system dominated the agricultural production, eventually forcing the large sections of the peasantry into drudgery

• Another dimension of agriculture planning with respect to policy making was the absence of a link between the agricultural production and the distribution patterns. Therefore, amazingly one notices that in spite of the remarkable increase in the production of even food grains (which might perhaps suffice to feed the entire population), still majority population is left without sufficient benefits owing to this increase

- The emphasis on an urban oriented agricultural production system has made agriculture dependent on industries and businesses that are controlled by the urban based elite. Therefore, a small section of the farming community has benefitted from agriculture while remaining vast majority of the community has been alienated from the urban market opportunities.

The differential levels of land reform have affected the agriculture production directly. The Committee to review the existing administrative arrangements for rural development and poverty alleviation programs (1985) noted that in large tracts of the country, the first stage land reforms (in the form of distribution of land to the tillers) were yet to be completed. Indeed, in these regions the major part of agricultural land was cultivated by bigger land owners in a very inefficient manner. In the rest of the country, the second stage land reforms (in the form of more efficient land utilization and land management) were being called for - which even now is still a distant dream. The second stage land reforms can be accomplished only after a more balanced distribution and utilization of irrigation is adopted (the combined report by the World Bank and Government of India highlights the challenges posed by the conditions emerging from The New Economic Policy of India and the World Agricultural Trade Liberalization on Indian agricultural economy. It mentions that **the expected growth rate for Indian agriculture at present is 4.5% as against its historical record of 3%. Such an enhanced agricultural performance would be possible only if there is an augmentation of productivity and a more diversified and higher – value farm production, and that can happen mostly within the irrigation sector**).

Appendix 2

Table 2.1: Different Completed, On-going and Proposed Irrigation Projects in the State of Maharashtra

Sr. No.	Region	Large	Medium	Minor	Irrigation Potential	Cultivable Land	Geographical Area
		No.	No.	No.	100,000 Ha.	100,000 Ha.	100,000 Ha.
1	Konkan	7	21	335	2.60	15.28	30.79
2	Nashik	16	76	560	14.30	40.18	58.76
3	Pune	29	45	995	16.31	39.93	57.59
4	Marathwada	12	83	625	12.10	47.45	64.30
5	Amravati	8	36	544	7.65	32.04	45.97
6	Nagpur	17	71	472	10.68	24.50	51.27
7	**Total**	**89**	**332**	**3,531**	**63.64**	**199.38**	**308.59**

Table 2.2: Operational Landholdings and Their Areas in Maharashtra for 1990 – 91

Sr. No.	Size of Holding	Number of Holdings		Operational Area		Average Size of Holding
		100,000 Ha.	Percentage (%)	100,000 Ha.	Percentage (%)	Ha.
1	Marginal up to 1 Ha.	32.75	34.58	16.18	7.73	0.49
2	Small 1 – 2 Ha.	27.27	28.80	39.83	19.03	1.46
3	Semi Medium 2 – 4 Ha.	21.26	22.45	58.80	28.10	2.77
4	Medium 4 – 10 Ha.	11.71	12.37	68.56	32.76	5.85
5	Large above 10 Ha.	1.71	1.81	25.80	12.37	15.13
6	**Total Classes**	**94.70**	**100**	**209.25**	**100**	**2.21**

Table 2.3: Region wise Distribution of Land, Rural Population and Irrigated Area

(a) Population composition

Sr. No.	Region	Number of Districts	Total Population (persons)	Rural Population (persons)	Total Workers (persons)	Agricultural Workers (persons)
			100,000	100,000	100,000	100,000
1	Konkan	5	193.76	55.27	74.53	16.76
2	Nashik	4	129.48	96.5	57.47	38.66
3	Pune	5	164.05	110.74	69.63	36.49
4	Marathwada	7	128	99.99	57.57	41.1
5	Amravati	4	91.64	62.81	38.46	28.09
6	Nagpur	5	90.21	58.65	38.46	23.36
	Total	**30**	**797.14**	**483.96**	**336.12**	**184.46**

(b) Area composition

Sr. No.	Region	Total Geographical Area	Forest Area	Wasteland	Net Sown Area	Pressure on Land
		100,000 Ha.	100,000 Ha.	100,000 Ha.	Ha.	Ha/capita
1	Konkan	30.8	7.62	15.26	7.92	0.69
2	Nashik	48.67	14.08	8.46	36.13	1.56
3	Pune	57.58	8.94	11.63	37.01	1.81
4	Marathwada	63.92	5.17	10.95	48.2	3.73
5	Amravati	43.99	10.22	5.09	30.68	2.08
6	Nagpur	43.99	24.54	6.37	20.36	0.36
	Total	**288.95**	**70.57**	**57.76**	**180.3**	**10.23**

(c) Irrigated area

Sr. No.	Region	Percentage Irrigation	Net Area Irrigated	Area Required at 0.16 ha/capita	Additional Irrigation Area Required	Sugarcane Area
		%	100,000 Ha.	100,000 Ha.	100,000 Ha.	100,000 Ha.
1	Konkan	5.52	0.39	8.84	8.45	-
2	Nashik	16.21	6.14	15.44	9.30	1.28
3	Pune	18.47	6.76	19.15	12.39	2.63
4	Marathwada	13.49	6.57	15.99	9.42	1.43
5	Amravati	4.92	1.48	10.05	8.57	0.1
6	Nagpur	19.06	3.88	9.38	5.5	0.03
	Total	**12.94**	**25.22**	**78.85**	**53.63**	**5.47**

Table 2.4 (District wise Distribution of Land, Rural Population and Irrigated Area in Regions)

(A) Konkan

(a) Population composition

Sr. No.	District	Total Population (persons)	Rural Population (persons)	Total Workers (persons)	Agricultural Workers (persons)
		100,000	100,000	100,000	100,000
1	Gr. Mumbai	99.26	–	35.09	0.08
2	Thane	52.49	18.56	20.86	5.87
3	Raigad	18.25	14.96	7.97	4.51
4	Ratnagiri	15.44	14.06	6.82	4.23
5	Sindhudurg	8.32	7.69	3.79	2.07
	Total	**193.76**	**55.27**	**74.53**	**16.76**

(b) Area composition

Sr. No.	District	Total Geographical Area	Forest Area	Wasteland Area	Net Sown Area	Pressure on Land
		100,000 Ha.	100,000 Ha.	100,000 Ha.	100,000 Ha.	100,000 Ha.
1	Gr. Mumbai	0.38	0.02	0.36	–	–
2	Thane	9.34	4.61	2.05	2.68	0.2
3	Raigad	6.87	2.26	2.78	1.83	0.14
4	Ratnagiri	8.17	0.26	5.56	2.35	0.18
5	Sindhudurg	6.04	0.47	4.51	1.06	0.17
	Total	**30.8**	**7.62**	**15.26**	**7.92**	**0.69**

(c) Irrigated Area

Sr. No.	District	Percentage Irrigation	Net Area Irrigated	Area Required at 0.16 ha/capita	Additional Irrigation Area Required	Sugarcane Area
		%	100,000 Ha.	100,000 Ha.	100,000 Ha.	100,000 Ha.
1	Gr. Mumbai	–	–	–	–	–
2	Thane	2.43	0.07	2.97	2.9	–
3	Raigad	5.46	0.1	2.39	2.29	–
4	Ratnagiri	0.85	0.02	2.25	2.23	–
5	Sindhudurg	18.87	0.2	1.23	1.03	–
	Total	**5.52**	**0.39**	**8.84**	**8.45**	–

(B) Nashik

(a) Population composition

Sr. No.	District	Total Population (persons)	Rural Population (persons)	Total Workers (persons)	Agricultural Workers (persons)
		100,000	100,000	100,000	100,000
1	Nashik	38.51	24.82	16.88	10.73
2	Dhule	25.36	20.16	11.51	7.82
3	Jalgaon	31.88	23.13	13.66	9.52
4	Ahmednagar	33.73	28.39	15.42	10.59
	Total	**129.48**	**96.5**	**57.47**	**38.66**

(b) Area composition

Sr. No.	District	Total Geographical Area	Forest Area	Wasteland Area	Net Sown Area	Pressure on Land
		100,000 Ha.	100,000 Ha.	100,000 Ha.	100,000 Ha.	100,000 Ha.
1	Nashik	15.63	3.64	2.99	9	0.37
2	Dhule	4.38	6	0.99	7.39	0.37
3	Jalgaon	11.64	2.24	1.26	8.14	0.38
4	Ahmednagar	17.02	2.2	3.22	11,6	0.44
	Total	**48.67**	**14.08**	**8.46**	**36.13**	**1.56**

(c) Irrigated area

Sr. No.	District	Percentage Irrigation	Net Area Irrigated	Area Required at 0.16 ha/capita	Additional Irrigation Area Required	Sugar-cane Area
		%	100,000 ha.	100,000 ha.	100,000 ha.	100,000 ha.
1	Nashik	14.78	1.33	3.97	2.64	0.23
2	Dhule	10.28	0.76	3.23	2.47	0.17
3	Jalgaon	16.34	1.33	3.7	2.37	0.12
4	Ahmednagar	23.45	2.72	4.54	1.82	0.76
	Total	**16.21**	**6.14**	**15.44**	**9.3**	**1.28**

(C) Pune

(a) Population composition

Sr. No.	District	Total Population (persons)	Rural Population (persons)	Total Workers (persons)	Agricultural Workers (persons)
		100,000	100,000	100,000	100,000
1	Pune	55.33	27.26	22.07	9.34
2	Solapur	32.31	32.02	13.82	8.18
3	Satara	24.51	21.36	11.01	6.31
4	Sangli	22	17.07	9.46	5.47
5	Kolhapur	29.9	22.03	13.27	7.19
	Total	**164.05**	**119.74**	**69.63**	**36.49**

(b) Area composition

Sr. No.	District	Total Geographical Area	Forest Area	Waste-land Area	Net Sown Area	Pressure on Land
		100,000 Ha.	100,000 Ha.	100,000 Ha.	100,000 Ha.	100,000 Ha.
1	Pune	15.62	2.78	2.9	9.94	0.39
2	Solapur	15.01	1.12	2.64	11.25	0.55
3	Satara	10.58	2.36	2.52	5.7	0.3
4	Sangli	8.61	0.8	1.82	5.99	0.37
5	Kolhapur	7.76	1.88	1.75	4.13	0.2
	Total	**57.58**	**8.94**	**11.63**	**37.01**	**1.81**

(c) Irrigated area

Sr. No.	District	Percentage Irrigation	Net Area Irrigated	Area Required at 0.16 ha/capita	Additional Irrigation Area Required	Sugar-cane Area
		%	100,000 Ha.	100,000 Ha.	100,000 Ha.	100,000 Ha.
1	Pune	18.71	1.86	4.36	2..5	0.5
2	Solapur	16.89	1.9	5.12	3.22	0.64
3	Satara	23.16	1.32	3.42	2.1`	0.45
4	Sangli	15.69	0.94	2.73	1.79	0.49
5	Kolhapur	17.92	0.74	3.52	2.78	0.5
	Total	**18.47**	**6.76**	**19.15**	**12.39**	**2.58**

(D) Marathwada

(a) Population composition

Sr. No.	District	Total Population (persons)	Rural Population (persons)	Total Workers (persons)	Agricultural Workers (persons)
		100,000	**100,000**	**100,000**	**100,000**
1	Aurangabad	22.14	14.89	9.47	6.14
2	Jalana	13.64	11.34	6.57	4.95
3	Beed	18.22	14.95	8.55	6.06
4	Parbhani	21.17	16.4	9.64	7.18
5	Nanded	23.3	18.24	10.32	7.26
6	Osmanabad	12.76	10.82	5.75	4.33
7	Latur	16.77	13.35	7.27	5.18
	Total	**128**	**99.99**	**57.57**	**41.1**

(b) Area composition

Sr. No.	District	Total Geographical Area	Forest Area	Wasteland Area	Net Sown Area	Pressure on Land
		100,000 Ha.	100,000 Ha.	100,000 Ha.	100,000 Ha.	100,000 Ha.
1	Aurangabad	10.08	1.29	1.4	7.39	0.52
2	Jalana	7.73	0.44	1.45	5.84	0.6
3	Beed	11.17	0.66	2.39	8.12	0.62
4	Parbhani	10.98	0.78	1.81	8.39	0.55
5	Nanded	10.33	1.51	1.49	7.33	0.42
6	Osmanabad	7.35	0.19	1.46	5.7	0.58
7	Latur	6.68	0.3	0.95	5.43	0.44
	Total	**64.32**	**5.17**	**10.95**	**48.2**	**3.73**

(c) Irrigated area

Sr. No.	District	Percentage Irrigation	Net Area Irrigated	Area Required at 0.16 ha/capita	Additional Irrigation Area Required	Sugar-cane Area
		%	100,000 Ha.	100,000 Ha.	100,000 Ha.	100,000 Ha.
1	Aurangabad	13.26	0.98	2.38	1.4	0.27
2	Jalana	8.56	0.5	1.81	1.31	0.14
3	Beed	21.43	1.74	2.39	0.65	0.18
4	Parbhani	12.4	1.04	2.62	1.58	0.14
5	Nanded	7.64	0.56	2.92	2.36	0.15
6	Osmanabad	20.88	1.19	1.73	0.54	0.18
7	Latur	10.31	0.56	2.14	1.58	0.17
	Total	**13.49**	**6.57**	**15.99**	**9.42**	**1.43**

(E) Amravati

(a) Population composition

Sr. No.	District	Total Population (persons)	Rural Population (persons)	Total Workers (persons)	Agricultural Workers (persons)
		100,000	**100,000**	**100,000**	**100,000**
1	Buldhana	18.86	14.98	8.9	6.96
2	Akola	22.14	15.8	9.94	7.11
3	Amravati	22	14.83	9.78	6.57
4	Yevatmal	20.77	17.2	9.84	7.45
	Total	**91.64**	**62.81**	**38.46**	**28.09**

(b) Area composition

Sr. No.	District	Total Geogra-phical Area	Forest Area	Waste-land Area	Net Sown Area	Press-ure on Land
		100,000 Ha.	**100,000 Ha.**	**100,000 Ha.**	**100,000 Ha.**	**100,000 Ha.**
1	Buldhana	9.68	1.64	1.18	6.86	0.49
2	Akola	10.57	1.33	1.28	7.96	0.56
3	Amravati	10.22	3.96	1.03	7.23	0.52
4	Yevatmal	13.52	3.29	1.6	8.63	0.51
	Total	**43.99**	**10.22**	**5.09**	**30.68**	**2.08**

(c) Irrigated area

Sr. No.	District	Percentage Irrigation	Net Area Irrigated	Area Required at 0.16 ha/capita	Additional Irrigation Area Required	Sugarcane Area
		%	100,000 Ha.	100,000 Ha.	100,000 Ha.	100,000 Ha.
1	Buldhana	6.27	0.43	2.4	1.97	0.02
2	Akola	3.27	0.26	2.53	2.27	0.01
3	Amravati	6.22	0.45	2.37	1.92	0.01
4	Yevatmal	3.94	0.34	2.75	2.41	0.06
5	**Total**	**4.92**	**1.48**	**10.05**	**8.57**	**0.1**

(F) Nagpur

(a) Population composition

Sr. No.	District	Total Population (persons)	Rural Population (persons)	Total Workers (persons)	Agricultural Workers (persons)
		100,000	100,000	100,000	100,000
1	Wardha	10.67	7.84	4.8	3.34
2	Nagpur	32.87	12.56	12.26	4.94
3	Bhandara	21.08	18.32	10.51	6.96
4	Chandrapur	17.72	12.75	8.2	5.08
5	Gadchiroli	7.87	7.18	4.24	3.04
	Total	**90.19**	**58.65**	**40.01**	**23.36**

(b) Area composition

Sr. No.	District	Total Geographical Area	Forest Area	Wasteland Area	Net Sown Area	Pressure on Land
		100,000 Ha.	100,000 Ha.	100,000 Ha.	100,000 Ha.	100,000 Ha.
1	Wardha	6.29	1.18	0.7	4.41	0.53
2	Nagpur	9.57	2.93	1.11	5.53	0.45
3	Bhandara	9.28	4.19	1.56	3.53	0.22
4	Chandrapur	10.92	4.24	1.8	4.88	0.41
	Gadchiroli	14.92	12	0.93	4.99	0.32
	Total	**50.98**	**24.54**	**6.1**	**23.34**	**1.98**

(c) Irrigated area

Sr. No.	District	Percentage Irrigation	Net Area Irrigated	Area Required at 0.16 ha/capita	Additional Irrigation Area Required	Sugarcane Area
		%	100,000 Ha.	100,000 Ha.	100,000 Ha.	100,000 Ha.
1	Wardha	3.17	0.14	1.25	1.11	0.02
2	Nagpur	11.75	0.65	2.01	1.36	0.01
3	Bhandara	47.59	1.68	2.93	1.25	0.01
4	Chandrapur	18.85	0.92	2.04	1.12	–
5	Gadchiroli	24.62	0.49	1.15	0.66	–
	Total	**21.19**	**3.88**	**9.38**	**5.5**	**0.04**

Appendix 3

Pani Panchayat: The springboard for a sustainable development[vii]

Many traditional communities living in resource-poor areas, over the centuries, have learnt to live within the limits of availability of resources. Even though modern technological advances have made it easier to cope with water shortages, they have also served to deplete the resources at a faster rate. Men and women migrate to cities in order to escape the problems created by water shortages, little realizing that the problem will eventually catch up with them wherever they go. For it is no longer a rural problem alone, but is rapidly becoming a major urban problem as well.

With a sectorial approach to planning, considerable progress has taken place in industrial development and also in a few sectors of agriculture production. In agriculture, the thrust was towards improvement through the introduction of “Green Revolution”. The Green Revolution package included introduction of hybrid, high yielding, water intensive crops, fertilizers, pesticides etc. The heavy stress on high water consumption food grains resulted in the neglect of crops requiring less water. As a result, the productivity of rain-fed crops remained stagnant or even decreased in some areas.

Increasing population pressure on land, meagre irrigation potential (the limited irrigation mainly going to the Green Revolution Areas) has resulted in the degradation of the land. Thus, economic development, in the absence of social development, has resulted in unequal distribution of the benefits, despite the large allocation of money for poverty alleviation. What is needed is to create assets which are sustainable in the long run. In an agrarian economy like ours, we need to give protective irrigation for at least one growing season a year.

What happens when water is made available for irrigation? Does water resolve all problems of employment and food security? The Naigaon experiment leading into the Pani Panchayat movement was initiated by Vilasrao Salunkhe to answer these questions. The term Pani Panchayat actually refers to the mobilization of groups of farmers for the formulation and implementation of community irrigation projects. Today Pani Panchayat symbolizes the principle of equitable distribution of water. Indeed the concept and method of sharing water equitably is the biggest and main contribution of Pani Panchayat experiment to society. At a time when people were talking of mitigating inequalities through land distribution, Pani Panchayat showed that ‘allocation of basic minimum quantum of water to each family is the first step towards reducing inequalities among the rural poor, especially those who live in resource – poor areas by increasing the income levels of all tillers’.

Appendix 4

Miscellaneous notes:

These are some of the notes that were prepared during the course of the first drafting of the book. Many portions were kept out of the main body of the book in order to keep a focus on the exposition of roots of the problem of underperforming agriculture sector in India and then propose solution in the form of equity based use of land and water. In fact, the perspective put forth in the present appendix outlines the complex nature of Indian society which necessitates accounting of factors beyond conventional economics. Late Vilasrao was not in agreement with these principles, which became a point of serious disagreement between us, followed by my then decision to withdraw from publication of our book. Even today I think that the excerpts shared in this appendix help to understand the underside of the dogmas of economic growth based model of development even better. Notes below reflect the political, economic conditions of 1990s and certainly will not reflect the status of 2020. These notes are solely my responsibility and nobody else can be held responsible for them.

1. One feature common to different policy approaches is the disconnecting of water related issues from one of the equitable distribution of land and water. This structural loophole has a direct adverse consequence for the environment systems; realization of the goal of equitable distribution of land and water. On the other hand, it is deeply rooted in the growth oriented concept of development which implies use of the water resources for commercial agriculture; concentration of water and land in the hands of a small section of rich farmers; and socio-economic disparities at both micro level of villages and areas little above these and macro level of districts and regions. ...for example, the Sardar dam project ...is supposed to provide power support to the rapid and massive industrialization drive in Gujarat (and to a less extent in the state of Maharashtra). Even though the aim of garnering power support to the effort at industrialization is appreciable there are yet many complex moral and serious social issues involved in such type of project.

2. In Maharashtra, the average production of many crops is much less compared to other parts of the country. When compared with the two states of West Bengal and Kerala, the average agricultural production of Maharashtra is less than that of West Bengal and more than that of Kerala. But this does not reflect the state of management of water resources in either of the three. In West Bengal, agriculture is dependent on monsoon rains and perennial

water available in the Ganges and its tributaries. The same factors help the agriculture in Kerala which in fact have a major advantage of monsoon rains. However, the pressure on land must have reached a threshold in both the states sometime in the past which has prompted migration. In Kerala, the migration has helped to ease the pressure on land, while it persists in West Bengal.

3. All the major observers of development of irrigation have mentioned that India has achieved its potential for covering of area under irrigation. Except a few parts of the country, e.g. north-east India, the rest of the country has optimized the potential expansion. Three reasons offered for this are, namely, (a) fiscal and environmental costs projected for any expansion are on the higher side; (b) the competition for water from different spheres of society is increasing; and (c) the costs required to be spent on the maintenance of the current projects are on the higher side, yet they will have to be spent. One needs to look into the performance; and social and economic impact of the current projects in the light of this shift in thinking of the policy makers. The points to focus upon are

- Area targeted by the projects of different scales and the actual area they could cover
- Cropping patterns: have these become more sustainable?
- Equitable distribution of water
- Are there severe inter-regional disparities in the distribution of water?

4. The case study of Maharashtra may be reviewed in the context of the National Water Policy (1987) and the emerging trend of irrigation related thinking.

- In the year 1990, 20 % of total cultivable land was under double cropping
- In the same year, 15 % of total irrigated land was under double cropping
- Average crop production for Maharashtra is very less compared to the national average and other few states
- 60 % of total irrigation is available for sugarcane cultivation, which is not an essential agricultural item. The land under sugarcane is in the range of 3-4 % of total land under cultivation
- Green revolution restricted to certain pockets in the state
- Need for coordination of storage, distribution and use of water

- Food grains are not receiving protected irrigation, therefore, their production has remained more or less at the same level as in 1961-62

- Uneven distribution of rain in different parts of the state which is not flattened at the level of use of water through coordinated storage, distribution and use of water

- Expansion of irrigation does not guarantee availability of water to all. Major portion of the available irrigation is through groundwater sources. Only 15 % farmers are owner of these sources

- There is a reduction in the average landholding size of the state in the period 1980-97.

- The proportion of land under forest, wasteland, and cultivable land is drastically different for different districts of the state. The proportion of land under forest ranges from 3 % to 75 %. The total land under forest is 20 %. Large part of it is wasteland and thus unproductive.

- The same situation as above persists with respect to the land under cropping. It ranges from 30 % to 70 % in different districts of the state.

- Irrigation is available in extremely uneven proportion in different districts.

- There are more acute disparities in the utilization of water by different sections of the population as one move down from larger to smaller territories. Pune district is representative of this situation.

- 48 % of total cultivable land is possessed by 14 % landholders.

5. Did the British create a new system of land and water ownership and why did they do so?

(a) The pre-British period was characterized by a rudimentary presence of the centralized state at the local level. Though there is no doubt that the rulers in those times relied on revenues collected from land and tributes from local lords in maintaining their own existence and running the administrative apparatus, yet this was a function done indirectly through local agents, mostly the local landlords. Under this system, land was owned by the individual landlords and they used the labor of the tenants to cultivate the land. The tenancy rights of the farmers were guaranteed through the local patronage of the landlord. This landholding and revenue system existed in most parts of the country with regional variants. There were regional peculiarities to be noticed, e.g. the tank irrigation system in south India which is reputed to be a community managed affair. These or the groupings of farmers to dig wells and channels for collective distribution of water were definite indicators of communal principles operating at local level. However, there is no doubt that these collective enterprises were always subordinated to the stratified social-political order which extended between the villages and floating centers of political power at the top of the hierarchy.

Agriculture under such system was overwhelmingly rain-fed. Besides that, the farmers relied on the surface water, provided by the rivers and the tributaries mainly for irrigation. The third important source of water for agriculture was the groundwater which used to be exploited through construction of wells. The fourth source of water supply, that is, canal irrigation was a much localized phenomenon. Though there have been mentions of small-scale canal irrigation systems having been in existence in some parts of the country, these were directly financed by the local landlords, and thus, controlled by them to serve their own land tracts. Once these canals became defunct due to deposit of silt; waterlogging; and increased salinity, they used to be abandoned. These conditions would be often put the Indian agriculture at the risk of the vicious cycle of famines. In the basin systems of big rivers, this cycle would be a pretty intricate pattern with flooding and dry spells alternating over long period till the normal conditions of cropping were resumed.

(b) Convenient revenue system?

The British political domination in the Indian sub-continent was consolidated after a long period of uncertainty. In the period immediately before the consolidation of the British power, the central power had weakened to such an extent that the local landlords were operating virtually as highly autonomous loci of economic and political power. Indeed it was the military and revenue support of the local landlords which would determine the viability of the political decisions made by the so-called central powers.

There was a sharp discontinuation of these patterns by the British. The motive for doing so was clearly rooted in the need for stabilization of a revenue system on which obviously they would have to rely for the survival of their political and economic domination. The British expected a revenue system that would provide them a direct control over the land and water resources. This implied a direct link between the farmer; the communities of the farmers and the rulers. This link was established through (i) institution of 'settlement' system for regularizing the land ownership patterns; (ii) creation of land records that provided a direct access to the information pertaining to agricultural produces and otherwise on all pieces of land; and (iii) consolidating control over land through land records and attaching lands not owned by individuals to the government. This direct link was forged through creation of bureaucracy that was loyal exclusively to the State. Under such system, even the landlords were subordinated to the will and dictates of the State.

Another development that provided a backdrop to the haste of the newly established colonial rule to expand the irrigation system were the recurrent famines that afflicted the large parts of the sub-continent over a period of almost two hundred years between the seventeenth and the nineteenth century. These famines had dilapidating effect on the Indian agriculture. If the situation would have continued unabated it could have led to a severe crisis for the economy based on agriculture. Therefore, even the urge shown by British government could be looked upon as an act of desperation to avert the potential crisis.

The upgrading of the water harvesting system and more particularly, improving the canal irrigation systems was born out of the motive to collect increasing revenues in order to meet the needs of the growing bureaucracy under the colonial rule. These changes that were induced by the colonial rule are well illustrated by the case study of the Indus Basin system (now in Pakistan). The region holds similarities with the rest of the Indian sub-continent with respect to social structure, cultural traditions, agro-climatic conditions, and history. The region belonged to the unified British Indian Imperial domain; therefore, its political history is very similar to the rest of the sub-continent.

There is a close connection between the generation and growth of the State in the colonial form; creation of the irrigation bureaucracy; subjection of the feudal system based on patriarchal values to the political-legal framework (which resulted into a shift from the patron-client relationship between landlords and tenants to the direct link between the individual farmer and the bureaucracy); and rapid expansion of the land under cultivation concomitant with the spread of irrigation; fragmentation of land into smaller units; induction of cash cropping as a substitute or supplement to subsistent agriculture (due to the requirement to meet the demands imposed by the colonial revenue system); and change in the structure of the Indian peasantry. This change with breakneck speed was topped by rapid growth in the population (Merry and Wolf, 1986).

The above case study helps to draw certain inferences with respect to the consequences of the augmentation of the colonial rule on the Indian agriculture sector and subsequently on the Indian social structure and economy. These are, namely

(i) Introducing the new revenue system and the emphasis on rejuvenation of dormant irrigation systems or their expansion were commonly motivated by the need to organize more stable channels of revenue collection. This motivation pushed the British to take up expansion of irrigation instead of improvement and maintenance of the already operational canals which left behind severe irrigation management problems for the newly independent continent.

(ii) The landlords responded to the land reforms by moving tenants out of the estates. The rest were reduced to wage laborers.

(iii)The possibility of bringing surplus land under irrigation stimulated landlords to either buy or extract landholdings from small farmers. The recurrent draughts (due to the unpredictable summer monsoon and / or improper water supply as a result of the failures of the irrigation systems) would accentuate this process of concentration in the hands of the landlords.

(iv) Uneven distribution of irrigation led towards a spurt in commercialization of agriculture as certain areas benefitted from intense irrigation; and the areas marginally benefitting from irrigation farmers adopted a mixed cropping system.

(c) Carrying forward the colonial legacy

The irrigation policy led down by the British was continued with little modifications by the government of independent India. Therefore, the social and economic consequences of the policy remained or rather were accentuated in the post – independence period. The major features of irrigation development in independent India are

1. Thrust on expansion of irrigation. Therefore, there was a major investment in construction of major irrigation projects almost till the formulating of the IX Five Year Plan.

2. The irrigation systems created by the British were maintained without modifications in their respective capacity and functions.

3. There is a massive growth in the irrigation bureaucracy and increasing use of complex technology imposing escalating costs on the State for maintenance of the irrigation infrastructure.

4. Designs of the irrigation systems so far created by the State have been the brainchild of the engineers who looked into the technical efficiency of the projects than the suitability of the designs to the local conditions.

5. Manifold increase in the area under irrigation has helped the country to become self – sufficient with respect to food grains. The food crops that have benefitted the most from this process are wheat and rice. However, in spite of the heroic feats accomplished by the Green Revolution, the risks to the food

security of the country are calculated high as there are serious doubts regarding the retention of the satisfactory irrigation potential of the existing projects.

6. The geographical areas of the country that fell under the category of plains have mostly benefitted from the irrigation expansion. Perhaps, the north – east parts of the country are yet to witness a considerable development of its irrigation potential.

7. Irrigation has been distributed inequitably between regions; command areas of irrigation projects and different class of the society. This has shaped the pattern of distribution of economic benefits of development. Though no doubt that the expansion of irrigation has generated employment in various economic sectors directly and indirectly; still in many parts of the country the inequitable distribution of water and land has led to a sharp polarization of society into exclusive segments with respect to control and access to economic benefits.

Through expansion of the irrigation infrastructure, the British rule encouraged the strengthening of the position of the traditional landlords as well as initiated the emergence of a new class of farmers with stakes in commercial agriculture (which is possible only through intense irrigation). In some instances, the traditional landlords have transformed themselves into commercial agriculturalists. These are (in the past they were) the social elements that have a stake in a state of unequal distribution of land and water resources. They have always been looked upon as political allies by the rulers in the country since the nineteenth century.

Bibliography:

1. Asian Drama – an enquiry into the poverty of nations; by Gunnar Myrdal; Twentieth Century Fund; 1968

2. Bourgeois Politics of the Working Class; Economic and Political Weekly, Vol. 15, No.2 (January 12, 1980)

3. Development Perspectives for the 1980s; by S. C. Dube; Abhinav; New Delhi; 1983

4. Merry, D.J. et al; 1986a. Reorganizing irrigation: Local Level Management in the Punjab (Pakistan), in Irrigation Management in Pakistan; International Irrigation Management Institute; Colombo, Sri Lanka

5. Development Planning – the Indian experience by Sukhamoy Chakravarty; Oxford, Clarendon Press; 1987

6. The impact of development strategies on the rural poor : second analysis of country experiences in the implementation of the WCARRD programme of Action; Food and Agriculture Organization; 1988

7. The Good Society: The Pani Panchayat Model of Sustainable Water Management; by Ganesh Pangare and Vasudha Lokur; INTACH; 1996

8. The Road from Rio – sustainable development and the nongovernment movement in The Third World; by Julie Fisher; PRAEGER; 1993

9. State of India's Environment – A Citizen's Report; Edited by Anil Agarwal and Sunita Narain; Centre for Science and Environment; New Delhi; 1991

10. Results of Irrigation Management Transfer in the Columbia Basin Project, USA; by Mark Svendsen and Douglas L. Vermillion; International Irrigation Management Institute; Colombo; 1996

11. Report of the Working Group on Participatory Irrigation Management Programme for the IX Five Year Plan; Government of India, Ministry of Water Resources, Command Area Development Wing.

---

[i] Unpublished paper "The imbalance in the distribution of income and property in India" by Dr. Nilkanth Rath

[ii] The status of forest cover in the same districts in 2013 is as given here. Ratnagiri 51.13 %, Solapur 0.31 %, Jalna 0.84 %, Parbhani 0.79 %, Beed 1.64 %, Osmanabad 0.57 %, Latur 0.07 %, Sindhudurg 51.13 %, Sangli 1.69 %, Aurangabad 5.51 %, Buldhana 6.11%, Nagpur 20.43 %, Bhandara 24.72 %, Chandrapur 35.59 %, Gadchiroli 70.05%

[iii] It was 21.35 % of total water use in Maharashtra in 2018 (Water productivity cropping of major Indian crops, NABARD, 2018)

[iv] The number of operative sugar factories in Maharashtra was 188 in the year 207-18

[v] Figures for 1994-95

[vi] The new vision considers man, society and nature as elements in an integrated whole. According to this view, the interaction between man and nature is mediated through society, therefore, more integrated and harmonious the organization of human society, it increases the potential for a creative and harmonious relationship between man and nature. The need to establish these patterns in human society is expressed by Capra when he says,"...reconnecting with the web of life means building and nurturing sustainable communities in which we can satisfy our needs and aspirations without diminishing the chances of future generations...we can learn valuable lessons from the study of ecosystems, which are sustainable communities of plants, animals, and micro-organisms...we need to revitalize our communities – including our educational communities, business communities, and political communities - so that the principles of ecology become manifest in them as principles of education, management and politics." (Capra, Fritzof, 1996)

[vii] The detailed case study of Pani Panchayat project is included in 'Group Communication – Theory and Methods' by Sandeep Deshmukh, Ane Books India, New Delhi (2008).

www.ingramcontent.com/pod-product-compliance
Ingram Content Group UK Ltd.
Pitfield, Milton Keynes, MK11 3LW, UK
UKHW061538190726
13845UKWH00031B/1107

9 789354 193316